For Marilyn

Harold Knoll

Sailing Around the World the Wrong Way

Volume V

Turkey to the Black Sea

by
Harold Knoll, Jr.
with **Harold Byler, Jr.**

authorHOUSE™

1663 LIBERTY DRIVE, SUITE 200
BLOOMINGTON, INDIANA 47403
(800) 839-8640
WWW.AUTHORHOUSE.COM

First published by AuthorHouse 07/26/05

ISBN: 1-4208-4964-6 (sc)

Printed in the United States of America
Bloomington, Indiana

This book is printed on acid-free paper.

Table of Contents

Volume V

Volume VI

Dedicated to:

Harold and Edith Knoll
and
George and LaVonne Visser

ACKNOWLEDGEMENTS

Thanks to the following whose encouragement and support

have been very much appreciated

My wife Vondalee

My parents, Harold and Edith

My wife's parents, George and LaVonne Visser

My crewmembers and the many wonderful people whom I have met and invited on board for meals and shared stories

All the wonderful people around the world who gave us rides, cars and bicycles to use, and above all, friendship and advice

PREFACE

This book is the story of Captain Harold Knoll's voyage around the world. Captain Knoll is a unique individual; he not only has the dreams that most of us have but also has the fortitude and perseverance to attempt to implement his dreams. As a retired schoolteacher, he has knowledge of geography and history. But uniquely, he has the desire to explore that geography and history in person. Captain Knoll, by virtue of extensive study and experience, is a competent sea captain. He has, so far, spent ten years in his quest to sail around the world and has accomplished about one-quarter of his goal. Four previous volumes described the first four parts of his voyage. The fifth part of his voyage is described in this Volume V. Succeeding parts of his voyage will be described in future volumes.

I first met Harold on the island of Martinique in the Caribbean. I later joined him to sail the North Sea, the Mediterranean Sea, the Aegean Sea, and the Black Sea. He is not only a good captain but is also a very good companion. This is a necessary trait on a small sailboat. We never have had an argument. As a result, he has asked me to assist him in publishing his journals. As a personal friend and a long time sailor, I could not refuse. This story is presented in the manner in which it unfolds in Harold's journals.

This book is intended to be a guide to what aspiring world sailors can expect in strange foreign ports and to enhance their understanding and enjoyment of these places.

Harold Byler, Jr.
January 27, 2005
Brady, Texas

INTRODUCTION

As a young man, I spent years reading stories and looking at pictures of adventures around the world. The National Geographic and later Cruising World, along with various travel lectures, whetted my appetite for travel and adventure. To see new places with different races and colors of people with strange languages became a dream that I actively planned for, saved for, and plotted to achieve.

In high school and college I took courses in French, mathematics, electronics, etc. which were not required for my chosen BA degree in education. My advisors asked how these courses pertained to my educational goals. They did not understand that my hidden goal was to gain all the knowledge and skills necessary to sail around the world. They would have thought I was crazy!

I had another goal that was not too well thought out. That goal was to sire a dozen children. It would not have taken much thought to reveal the fact that "going away sailing" and "raising children" were totally incompatible. Sailing requires freedom from the responsibilities of home, wife, family, and job. Raising a large family requires a large home, a dedicated wife, and a job with a substantial income.

With two occupations, teaching school and farming, I was able to raise eight of my own plus several foster children. This kept me anchored at home with very little time for adventure. I had intended to start my big adventure around middle age, 45-50. However, I married for a second time to a younger woman with three cute little ones. This was poor planning on my part but an adventure in itself! By the time we had raised all of the children, I found myself at age sixty with a mind ready to travel but a body that was a little less willing to climb mountains, dive for lobster, or hike a rainforest.

Before tying the knot for the second time, I did ask some critical questions. Do you like the water? Yes! Would you like to sail? I think so! Would you go around the world? Sure, why not! I not only asked questions but I tested the waters. She liked to swim, fish, and boat. We went out in the worst storms in the smallest boat that I could find. My future wife was calmer, more collected, and less subject to panic than I was. She showed a tendency to take over as Captain while I knelt in the bilge bailing like mad to stay afloat!

During the first year of our marriage, my wife bought me a small 8-foot sailboat called a "Snark". She had watched me for some time sailing an old homemade vessel that was more submarine than sailboat. I had spent more time in the water than on deck. The slightest mistake resulted in a dunking in polluted Lake Macatawa near Holland, Michigan. I learned to tack, jibe, trim sail and most of the basics of sailing with very little help other than the knowledge that to make a mistake was to be tossed into the cold, muddy water. I learned fast under these conditions. The Snark, a foam and fiberglass wonder, proved to be an improvement. It was faster, better equipped, and more seaworthy. It was much drier but still willing to toss me overboard for the slightest transgression. I learned a lot more about sailing from the Snark.

Next came an old Catalina 22. Compared to the Snark, it was a dreamboat with a small cabin containing all the conveniences of home: a stove, sink, water tank, and porta-potty. Now my wife and girls took a real interest in sailing and we spent many days and nights aboard. Things were crowded but happy! Figure 1 is a picture of my Catalina 22.

The next logical decision was to invest heavily in a good sailboat capable of going out for long trips and eventually around the world. I sold property and saved for a down payment. In February of 1988, we spent a weekend at the Chicago Boat Show. We fell in love with and purchased a "Gulf 32" motorsailer made by Capital Yachts in California. We found out later that

Figure 1
My Catalina 22

the company was going bankrupt. We became owners of a big, heavy, fully equipped sailboat with a large 40-hp diesel engine. A description of this sailboat appears at the end of this introduction.

In talking with fellow sailors about routes around the world, it soon became evident that my ideas were different from those of most people. My plan started with the normal route of going south down the rivers to the Gulf. From this point on, I chose to depart from the norm and take the "wrong way around" according to the wise men of the marina set. The reasoning for the conventional route is based on the prevailing east winds. It is, of course, more difficult and slower to sail against the wind. However, I had no intention of risking my boat and my life crossing the Atlantic against the prevailing winds. My plan included a freighter ride across the Atlantic to Europe for my boat and me.

From Florida, I planned to visit the Bahamas, Hispaniola, Haiti, the Dominican Republic, Puerto Rico, the West Indies to Trinidad, and then to cross the Atlantic to Europe. I planned to explore the British Isles, Scandinavia, the European Continent, and then travel the Mediterranean Sea, the Aegean Sea, and the Black Sea. I wanted to visit Spain, France, Italy, Greece, Turkey, and the East Mediterranean countries, then go down through the Suez Canal and continue eastward.

Retirement couldn't come soon enough! At 60 years of age, the incentive of a lump-sum buyout pushed me over the rough spots and the decision was made. Goodbye home – bring on the world! In September of 1995, we traveled down Lake Michigan from our new home in Montague, MI, to explore the world! Volumes I, II, III, and IV cover the succession of trips from Lake Michigan, U.S.A., to Turkey. The route covered by this Volume V is shown in Figure 2 on the next page.

Figure 2
Map – Travel in the Black Sea

My Sailboat, the "Idyllic"

"Idyllic" is a hard name for Americans to pronounce and use. The French call it "Edillic". The English use it often in conversation and do not have any problem whatsoever with it. Figure 3 shows a picture of "Idyllic" being tied up by my wife and her father at his dock for the first time. Figure 4 shows "Idyllic" at her home mooring in Lake Macatawa at sunrise.

"Idyllic" is a Gulf 32 motorsailer with 32 feet overall length and a 10-foot beam. She has a low cabin roof and good sailing characteristics. This is a heavy displacement boat with a full keel. It displaces 7.5 tons with about 3.5 tons in the keel. It sails a little slow with light winds but is very upright and keeps a good course. The rig is a sloop with a two-reef mainsail, working jib, 150% genoa with Harken roller furling, and a small storm sail. At first I planned on converting it to a cutter rig but found this unnecessary, especially in strong winds where I very seldom even use the mainsail.

A large 40-hp Universal diesel engine weighs the stern down slightly more than desirable but comes into its own on the rivers and canals of the US and Europe. It starts and runs great, is very economical and reliable.

The cabin below contains sleeping space for six. There is a double-vee berth in the bow that is shown in Figure 5, a berth partially under the starboard cockpit, a settee berth and a table which folds up to create a double berth in the main saloon which is shown in Figure 6. Figure 7 shows the inside helm.

Figure 3
"Idyllic" at the dock for the first time

Figure 4
"Idyllic" at her home mooring

Figure 5
"Idyllic" Vee- Berth below

Figure 6
"Idyllic" Main Saloon

Figure 7
"Idyllic" Inside Helm

There is a full galley with a CNG cook stove that was later converted to butane (called camping gaz in Europe). There is a hot (manifold) and cold water system in the galley and in the head that contains a lavatory, shower and toilet. This toilet is the most disagreeable appliance on board in terms of maintenance. There is also a freshwater shower in the cockpit. The freshwater tank holds 75 gallons, which is enough for 4 people for a week if used carefully. The diesel fuel tank holds 75 gallons, which on some occasions is too much fuel storage. However, this is a valued asset when running the motor full time on canals and rivers.

The boat has wheel steering with an Auto Helm 4000 system. Her electronics include two GPS's, a big Garmin 75, and a small Magellan Pioneer that I found to be very adequate, extremely accurate, and reliable until it was submerged, taken through the German metal detectors and subjected to the Y2K disruptions. There is a VHF radio permanently mounted below by the chart table. I now have a small, handheld VHF that can be taken to the cockpit for convenience.

There are a lot of things I would like that come to mind such as an electric anchor winch, a bimini, additional anchors, passerelle, radar, and several 220v appliances to name a few. I'm on a retired man's budget and cannot buy everything I need at once. Some parts become worn out and obsolete and I now find myself replacing various things such as the autopilot, toilet, lights, sails, lines, dinghy, dinghy motor, etc., etc. She's a demanding mistress! But she's the love of my life. She's always ready to go, always there for me, and full of happiness and fun. There are many fond memories of past experiences with a treasured lover and friend! Figure 8 shows the "Idyllic" hull and sail plan. Figure 9 shows the deck and cabin plan. Figure 10 is a side view of the "Idyllic"'s sister ship. Figure 11 is a stern view of the same ship.

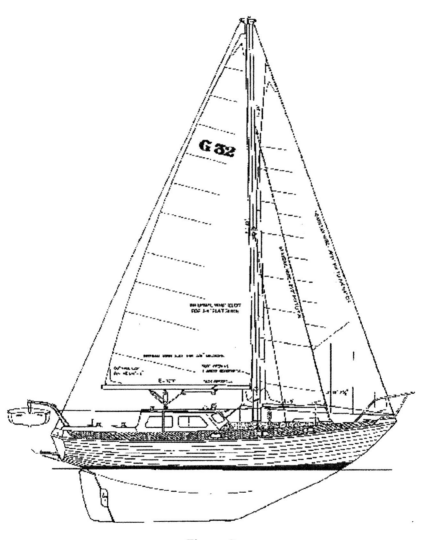

Figure 8
"Idyllic" Sail and Hull Plan

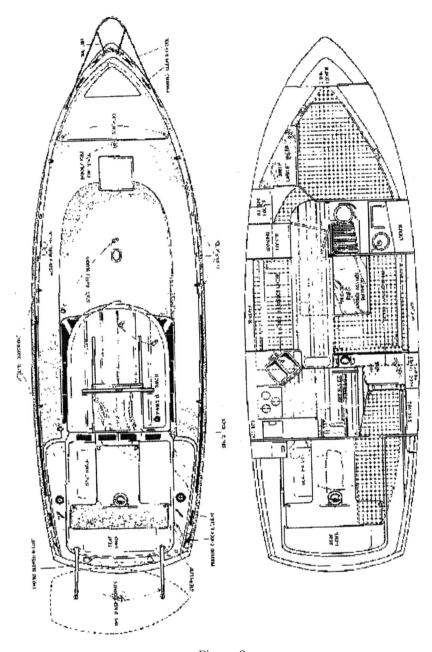

Figure 9
"Idyllic" Deck and Cabin Plan

Figure 10
Side View of "Idyllic" sister ship

Figure 11
Stern View of "Idyllic" sister ship

CHAPTER IX – 2004 THE BLACK SEA

Michigan to Yalikivak, Turkey

My flight from Detroit took me to Amsterdam, Netherlands, where I changed planes for a flight to Istanbul, Turkey. On Tuesday, June 1, 2004, I arrived in Istanbul where I stood in line at Passport Control until I was turned away because I didn't have a visa. After obtaining a visa for only $20 USD I stood in line again; last year the visa cost me $100 USD. Then I stood in line at the bank to cash some traveler's checks and waited for a half-hour while the teller did his security checks and paperwork, an unbelievably slow and cumbersome process. In the airport I was constantly accosted by salespersons for every product known to man.

Finally I called the Avis Travel and Tourism Agency that had a manager who spoke perfect English. I was very tired from the jet lag so I chose a relatively low-priced hotel that had free transportation from the airport. This three-star hotel cost me 92 million liras. At 1,260,000 to the US dollar, this was about $75 USD. The "Sport Hotel" was downtown in the Sultanahmet District right in the center of the main tourist attractions: the Grand Bazaar, the Egyptian bazaar, the Blue Mosque, the Hagia Sophia, and the Queen's Palace. The rooms were old but very clean. The hotel was frequented by mostly businessmen. After a shower I took a short nap.

The next morning, I discovered that breakfast was included in the price of the room. I expected coffee and a roll but discovered that it was an "all you can eat" buffet in the roof top dining room with bread, eggs, cheese, olives, tomatoes, and several delicious varieties of drinks. I found a small table in the corner with a beautiful wide view of the Maranara

1

Deniz (Sea of Maranara) and the freighter anchorage where fifty or more ships were anchored. Figure 12 shows the view from the rooftop dining room in the hotel. A short distance away in the rooftop restaurant was a seedy-looking chap in a black tank top with a body covered by tattoos and obviously not Turkish. I tried not to make eye contact as he was counting out a large pile of money that I assumed was for some kind of illegal undercover operation. The next thing I knew, he said "hello" with an Aussie accent and started to point out Princess Island that had the largest wooden house in the world and then the different sections of Istanbul in some detail. Despite my reluctance, he gained my interest but not my trust. Eventually I found out that he owned several companies that buy and sell heavy equipment in Georgia, Russia, Azerbaijan, Turkistan, and as he put it, "the whole bloody region". He ordered six Caterpillar bulldozers during the course of our conversation. The phone calls came and went all morning as we sat there talking. He was busy but couldn't resist showing me around town. We traveled fast and he gave a running account of every neighborhood and historical site so as to acquaint me with the town and orient me to locations for future visits. His name was Gary Dunn and he owned The Triquest Company. He was one of many helpful friends that I've met during my years of travel. Some of the things that we saw are shown in Figures 13 through 16.

The hotel gave me a free ride to the bus terminal (otogar) but would have charged me 5M TL to take me inside the square mile of the bus company complex. I walked in with my heavy suitcase. The scene was chaotic with all of the travel agent's salesmen.

I checked the prices of a few buses to Yalikavak, which ranged from 30 to 40M TL. Two distinguished looking men in white shirts and ties offered me tickets for 20M TL. I purchased a ticket from them and was

Figure 12
View from top of Sport Hotel

Figure 13
Istanbul Plaza in Sultanahmet District

Figure 14
Gate in Istanbul

Figure 15
Spice booths in the Egyptian Baazar

Figure 16
Turkish boy dressed up

led to a KAMIL KOC bus, only to be charged another 25M TL for a seat! Figure 17 shows the bus on the ferry ride from Istanbul across to the southern mainland. After a half-hour and six stops on the road, a bus official looked at my ticket. When I told him I wanted to go to Yalikavak, he told me that I was on the wrong bus and was going to Ankara.

He led me to the office where the manager explained that the two distinguished gentlemen who sold me the tickets were hucksters and that I had taken baksheesh (a bribe) illegally. I was required to buy another ticket. Meanwhile the driver, who must have been in on the deal, slipped back to me the 25M TL that he had charged me so that I wouldn't complain about him. It was necessary to wait several hours for the bus to Yalikavak.

While waiting, I decided to have lunch. I ordered a meat dish and got something that looked like tripe. While I was eating, some students from the university heard about my problem and asked to interview me on television. They questioned me about how I liked the bus station, Istanbul, and the town, Harmen, which I was in. Then they warned me that the area was particularly dangerous and to watch my bags carefully. Figure 18 shows the TV interview. I left the bags with the restaurant owner for safekeeping and went out to have a look around.

The bus ride from Istanbul to Yalikavak took 12 long hours to cross from Northern Turkey to Southern Turkey. The highways were modern and lined with up-to-date homes and businesses. The bus stations were modern, clean, and complete with rest rooms, food, and souvenir shops available. The very modern bus had two attendants in addition to the driver. Snacks and drinks were served from a bar at regular intervals and were available at all times. A John Wayne movie was shown in Turkish, which I thoroughly enjoyed. This took four hours to show as it was turned off at the bus stops.

The countryside consisted of low mountains separated by valleys several miles across. Every square inch of these valleys was cultivated with orchards, grain, and vegetable farms. There were olive trees everywhere. At one point I saw a stork on a chimney that I thought was probably a fake. It looked too real to be true but later I saw one feeding its babies and then some more feeding in a shallow lake.

The bus line stopped in Bodrum. I was transferred "free-on-board" to a dolmus (small van bus) going to Yalikavak where I took a taxi to the Tokar boat yard where I had left the "Idyllic" the previous year. I arrived to a warm reception and was given Turkish hugs with kisses on both cheeks by all on hand. My boat, "Idyllic", seemed to be in good shape except for a layer of sawdust and wood shavings from the gullet (type of large Turkish sailboat) being restored nearby. Figure 19 shows the gullet being restored nearby. In prior years, "Idyllic" had not always been

Figure 17
Ferryboat ride

Figure 18
TV interview

in good shape after winter storage. Figure 20 shows a fishing boat being repaired near "Idyllic".

I spent a miserable night trying to sleep. Due to jet lag I was wide-awake. The mosquitoes were out looking for blood. I hid under the blankets for two hours, safe but too hot. Finally I got up and found a breeze coming in the companionway. I set a fan there and turned it on high. This blew the mosquitoes away and I stayed cool. I then slept soundly until 7:00 a.m.

I devoted the entire day of Saturday, June 5th, returning to retrieve my Travel Permit from Customs. I got an early start to avoid the heat and the crowds. As I was leaving the boatyard, I met Videt, the young yard worker, and through gestures he explained that his boss, Mohamet, needed to fill in some papers and stamp them to accompany my application for the return of my Travel Permit. Videt called Mohamet and he arrived a short time later. I was glad that he was not on one of his binges or it might have taken several days. His education level is very low, so I filled in the blanks on the form, copying from last year's form. He applied his official boat yard stamp and signature. I could have said that I was a terrorist on the form and he wouldn't have known the difference. He would have approved it. He told me to go to Bodrum for customs approval. This would require a hike of two miles to the bus, a 2M TL bus ride, and a one mile hike in Bodrum. I had heard that the customs office might be moved to Turgutries, so I checked at the Yalikavak Marina. They said go to Turgutries but that it was closed on Saturdays. So instead I went shopping at Migros, the big chain store, in Yalikavak.

After I returned to the boatyard, they told me to return to the marina and the office girl, who had all of the details, would be in at 11:00 a.m. She told me that I needed to go to Bodrum where they were open 24

Figure 19
Turkish gullet being repaired

Figure 20
Turkish fishing boat being repaired

hours each day. I had already spent all of my money and had heavy bags of groceries by then. I walked to the 3 Brothers Restaurant and asked Thomas Ishemeil to watch my bags and give me a loan of 40M TL which he was more than willing to do. I went to the customs office in Bodrum, filled in the paperwork, and was back at the boat with the Travel Permit by 3:00 p.m.

That night, I met my good friend, Bryan Stephens, the owner of Mavi Kus Resort. I had helped him moor his Turkish gullet during a windstorm last year. Bryan is one of many who have settled, married, and become dual citizens of Turkey and the UK.

On Sunday, I put up the mainsail and found some areas of concern that would need some repair soon. One batten has broken through on the end. Also, the very end of the foot was frayed and the layers of cloth were separating from wear. I guess that some wear and tear on the rigging and sails is to be expected after 16 years of use.

I walked to town and checked out my e-mail messages. I had two from home, one from Kate in Texas telling me that she had bought a house and would be unable to join me for the summer, and two others from Etienne trying out a new computer and address. He said that he would join me about June 15 to 20. I had met Etienne last fall in Yalikavak and he wanted to sail with me all summer. I had been worried about him as my letters had been returned unopened and I had not heard from him. He was a ski instructor in Switzerland, which seemed to me to be a little dangerous. I sent short messages to my family and friends at home to let them know that I was safe.

The next day, I washed the topside of the boat. It was easy to get rid of the grime and sawdust. I was worried that the fiberglass might be stained but apparently the wax coating protected it. This was much easier than the black pollution in Lake Michigan that ate right into the fiberglass. I walked to the local small, box-like, Turkish deli and bought a Coca Cola and a beer, which cost 9M TL. I only had 5M TL. I promised to return with the balance and the clerk agreed. Now I have credit at two places in town. I returned after restocking my bulging billfold with 40M TL and paid the balance, bought more bread, and a 12-pack of small bottles of water.

There was a terrible windstorm Wednesday night but I didn't have to worry about the anchor dragging as the boat was still on land. The howling of the wind in the rigging and trees around me was very loud and the boat shook and wiggled with every blast of wind. This would not have been startling if the boat had been in the water but 20 feet in the air, supported on top of five tree trunks, it was a little disquieting.

The previous night I had discovered that when I heard a mosquito whine above my head, I could duck under the covers and reach up with the can of Raid and spray him. This seemed to work well without having to spray the whole cabin. Wednesday night it didn't seem to work as well. When I turned on the light to investigate my failure, I discovered that, in the dark, I had grabbed the spray can of WD40 instead of the Raid.

I went to 3 Brothers, my favorite bar and restaurant, for a meal out. Figure 21 is a picture of the three waiters at the restaurant. I had a meal of leg of lamb that was not as well done as I would have liked. There was a new chef that I had not talked to previously. The cost of the meal and drinks came to 35M TL, which is good but higher than last year. Later a belly dancer arrived and a show began. A lot of pictures were taken and some were of me dancing with her, which seemed to entertain the patrons. Figure 22 shows one of those pictures. It was especially entertaining to my friend Kaahn who is an expert dancer and dances everywhere, even on the street and the beach. Figure 23 shows Kaahn dancing.

Figure 21
Tuna   Kaahn   Thomas
Waiters at the 3 Brothers Restaurant

Figure 22
Knoll dancing with friend

Figure 23
Kaahn dancing

Eviet returned from sick leave on Thursday and immediately indicated to me, by sign language, that he would launch the boat that day. I had been on my way to the market bazaar that is held on Thursdays; instead I made immediate preparations for launching. Everything has to go smoothly for a safe and successful launching. The boat yard workers put the sled under the boat and lowered the boat down onto it. Then they attached a long cable to the sled and slid it over logs across the boatyard, across the road, and to the edge of the water. They moved the logs from behind around to the front as they pulled the sled.

They slid it down into the water with a great splashing. Everything went fine except that the engine on the boat wouldn't turn over. I had checked it before we started and it worked fine. I finally discovered that the battery cable was loose. I tightened it and the engine started easily. I motored out and attempted to anchor, but the anchor kept dragging on the weed bottom. My friend, Nick the German, came over in his dinghy and helped me run a line to a large concrete block for a more permanent mooring while waiting for my crewmember, Etienne, to show up on about the 15 to 20th of the month.

I awoke the next morning to a nice sunny day with the air and water crystal clear. There was little or no wind. I could easily see the bottom with its sea grass and small fish feeding all around the boat. I pulled the anchor rode and found it badly chafed where it passed through the iron ring in the concrete anchor block.

I took the dolmus to Bodrum where I bought some vegetables and three meters of chain to use for attaching the rode to the iron ring. While I was there, I toured the Bodrum Cales (Castle) that had been built by the Knights of St. John. In the museum there, I saw a shipwreck, discovered at Marmiras, displayed with its cargo of broken glass of all shapes, sizes, and colors being shipped to glass factories in the Black Sea. Everything that had been on the ship for the long voyage in ancient times was also displayed. I ate a kebab at a local restaurant for 3.5M TL and returned home. When I stopped at the 3 Brothers for a Coke, Kaahn gave me one of their company's T-shirts.

Returning to the boat, I immediately jumped in for a short, cool, refreshing swim in the turquoise water. Then I seized two loops of the chain to the anchor rode and covered the connections with duct tape. After that I dove down and connected the chain to the iron ring in the anchor block. I had just settled down when the owner of the mooring came to claim his concrete block. I had been told that he would not be back until the end of the summer. Diving down again, I disconnected the chain from the block and motored over to the boatyard mooring that was a long four meters down. I couldn't reach it at first but when I put on the swim fins and carried the dinghy anchor with me, I went down fast. Secure again, I went to the local deli stall and bought a six-pack of Coke and a loaf of Turkish bread.

I started Saturday morning by cleaning the bright work. It was a pleasant job in the cool morning air. I walked two miles to the benzene (gas) station where I spent 26M TL for outboard gas and oil. While I was waiting for the dolmus for the return trip, a propane truck stopped and the driver offered me a free ride. I offered him a tip, but he refused it saying in Turkish, "It was appreciated but not necessary". We shook hands as I left his truck and I had found a new friend. He passes "Idyllic" every day and rings a bell on the way by. I expect the ride was dangerous as the propane tanks were rolling and bouncing around in the back of the truck. I can just see the news report now. "World sailor blown sky high by propane explosion!"

I spent the next day swimming and working on the boat. In the evening, I went out to eat at a Turkish restaurant that served meatball dinners for 5M TL. The dinner consisted of a plate of cucumbers, onions, and tomatoes mixed in olive oil with a loaf of grilled bread and a plate of raw onions and meatballs made of lamb and beef mixed and grilled. The meatballs were like little wieners and were very tasty. The meal was followed by a glass of Turkish tea. After dinner, I went to the RAHAT Bar, which caters to Englishmen, and watched the futbal game between England and France. Figure 24 is a picture of me at the bar.

On Tuesday, June 15th, I walked to town to visit the Yalikavak Internet Café where I e-mailed Bassem Shihan and Etienne de Bruyne. Bassem replied that he couldn't get a visa to the Ukraine without an invitation from a native. I wondered if I would have this same problem. The wind switched from the West to the North, went up to 35 knots, and continued increasing; a typical Meltemi storm. My mooring was secure consisting of a heavy mooring line to two giant metal anchors chained together. However, I saw a large Turkish gullet slowly dragging her anchor toward "Idyllic". I watched closely to see what would develop. There was only one crewman on board and he seemed to be trying to run another line to shore by rowing it over in a small tender. He was having a real fight against the wind and waves. He soon gave up and made an emergency call to the captain. Within an hour, several of the boat's crew showed up by car and taxi. After a struggle, another gullet lifted its anchor, ran a line to the other gullet and proceeded to pull it out of danger. The last that I saw of them, they were motoring across the bay to tie up to the city quay.

The next morning, I saw that the large gullet that broke loose was back safely moored next to her sister ship, Esmeralda II. I walked to town again to e-mail Bassem. He planned to join me on the 18th of July in Istanbul

Figure 24
Knoll at RAHAT Bar

and then crew for me until the 23rd of August when he plans to be back in Istanbul to meet his girlfriend there. Returning to the boat, I went for a long swim around "Idyllic" and saw a large school of big fish in the shade of the boat. The seas were perfectly calm and the water was crystal clear. The Meltemi storms sometimes come and go very quickly in otherwise sunny clear weather. In fact, clear, sunny weather with very low humidity is usually the only warning of an approaching Meltemi.

Bryan stopped by with a warm, freshly baked loaf of Turkish bread and gave me welcome encouragement and reports on the weather. He was a bit down as the English lost to France in the futbal game the day before. We tested our radios and found both to be in perfect working order. This was the first for my new handheld radio. I later found it to be especially convenient when arriving in port.

Late in the evening just before retiring, I sat in the cockpit and admired the sky, the night lights, and the scenery. I could hear beautiful music coming from a hostel nearby. Looking through the binoculars, I could see young people playing a three-stringed instrument accompanied by hand drums. Men and women were singing, clapping, and dancing to the wonderful beat of the music. They were having a great time and, in the process, entertaining me also.

Thursday was market day again and I walked back to the boatyard with a full week's supply of groceries. I sat down to rest under the shade of a large fishing boat that was under repair there. Soon Mike, a Turkish born, former New York taxi driver, who was fluent in English, joined me. Then Roger, an Englishman living in the mountains behind town, joined us. Roger is the captain owner of "Orkin", a 60-year-old schooner moored in the harbor. In a short time, the owner of a fishing boat arrived and joined us. This boat was a trawler, the "B. Kardesler" of Kusadasi, Turkey.

I used Mike as an interpreter to ask the boat owner some questions. He said he would start fishing in another month when the season opened. He pays his crew a share of the profits from the fishing; the other captains pay $250 USD per month to their crews. Fishing has apparently been good the last few years as evidenced by the new van in which he drove up. He said that the quantity of fish had stayed the same or improved in each of the last years. "I make a good living", he said. "The government regulations are my biggest headache. Every year they make 5 to 20 new rules that I don't understand." He finds out about the new rules when he is given a ticket and has to pay a fine. Then he tries to avoid a repeat infraction.

I asked Mohamet, the boat yard owner, about charts for the Turkish coast once and he told me that they are not needed. He said, "All you have to do is follow the coast north or south", as he pointed each way. He had been sponge diving these waters with his father since he was a small boy. The sponges disappeared right after the nuclear explosion at Chernobyl in Russia, which was upwind of the prevailing northeast wind and up current above the Bosphorus and Dardanelles Strait.

On Saturday, I got an early start to the market to avoid the heat and the crowds. I was able to ride with Bryan who visits his boat once or twice every day to get away from his wife and to water down the deck boards to keep them from shrinking and causing leaks. Most wooden boat owners go through the same routine. I wash "Idyllic"'s fiberglass decks only to keep them clean.

At the market, I fondled the melons, tasted the olive varieties and the different cheeses. Figure 25 shows the marketplace. I bargained with the farmers and had a splendid time. My purchase of a kilo of plums brought the traditional response from the farmer. He took the money and threw it on the ground, picked it up, brushed it across his forehead, and then

Figure 25
Yalikavak farmer's market

stuffed it in his pocket. This tradition, Sivta or Sffte, is always done with the first sale of the day to bring good luck for the day's work.

I ran out of patience and wanted to get going although this place is very interesting and beautiful. The poet, Catullus, visiting near here in times past said about the resorts of Asia Minor, "Now the trepidation of departure, now the lust of travel, feet impatiently urging him be gone".

On Sunday, June 20th, an unusual storm blew up from the southwest exposing the north shore and the "Idyllic" to the full fury of the wind and the waves. The two gullets, Esmeralda I and II, were beginning to drag their anchors again while the "Idyllic" was banging away at the short mooring line. To prevent damage, I started the engine and put it in forward gear at idle speed to relieve the terrible jerking and pounding on the mooring line. The wind reached 50 knots and was gusting higher. I was glad that I had the new mooring line with the chain rode to the giant anchors that I had installed for just such an event.

While having tea with the Turkish Captain of the fishing boat, we both smelled smoke, but we couldn't discover the source. We were alarmed that anything would be burning in that high wind. Later, at 4:00 p.m., I again smelled smoke and this time I saw on the mountaintop to the south towards Bodrum a large billowing cloud of gray-black smoke rising skyward. This was the area where my friend, Roger, had his beautiful villa. Through the binoculars I could see fire blazing 50 feet into the air over a vast stretch in front of the mountains with the smoke being blown horizontally by the high winds. The temperature had stayed at 85 degrees Fahrenheit for a long time, and any rain that had fallen had immediately evaporated leaving tinder dry grass, brush, and pine forest.

Monday, June 21st, was cloudy with rain in the air and a cool breeze blowing from the southwest, which is a very unusual occurrence in this part of Turkey. There wasn't any sign of the fire or the storm except that the town was without electricity. Etienne, who was supposed to arrive by the 20th, still had not shown up.

The next day, I checked the E-mail without result. I watched the sun set in the west over the Greek mountains. The sky was bright red with just a dash of blue to set it off. While I was watching the beauty of the evening, Vidiet, the old Turkish ship's engineer, came along, said, "Hello", and we were off on an evening of seamen's tales of travel around the world; he, on a blue water freighter, and I on "Idyllic". Port by port, around the world, I soon found the night was late. On my way back to the boatyard, I stopped at the RAHAT Sports Bar where I was attracted by a futbal game between England and Latvia. England won and a pint of Effes beer later I headed out for "Idyllic", two kilometers away in the harbor.

Tuesday evening, as I was setting out for town, I met Evart, from the ship Viola, standing on the sea wall. Figure 26 is a picture of Evart on his boat "Viola". He was waiting for Bryan to come by so he could get a ride home. After talking for some time, I found out that he needed his dinghy taken to his home. It had been stolen by kids and dragged around until it got a puncture. It leaked air badly and needed repair. I agreed to carry it up the hill to his house, as it didn't appear to be too far. It was not too heavy but the road up the hill to his house was very steep. Evart was suffering from a dog bite and needed to go to Bodrum for rabies shots. Passing the neighborhood dogs on the way to his house, we had picked up stones to protect ourselves in the event of a dog attack. Loaded with the dinghy and stones, I arrived out of breath in front of his house.

His house was the typical three-story, whitewashed, box-style home found in this part of the world. He wanted the dinghy carried up to the third floor storeroom. I carried the dinghy up the steep, winding stairway.

Figure 26
Captain Evart on "Viola"

Since Evart lived on his boat most of the time, the third floor was used as a storeroom. The lower level was a nice apartment for his mother. It was very well furnished with modern conveniences. The appliances were apartment size. There was a patio overlooking the ocean and the mountains with a tremendous view of the harbor and "Idyllic" at her mooring. His rooftop patio had a 360-degree view of the harbor, the mountains of both Turkey and Greece, and the Aegean Sea. After watching the spectacular sunset into the sea, I was invited to eat dinner with the family. I protested since I was sure that his mother had not cooked food for company. My protest was weak as I dearly enjoy eating with local people to discover new foods and learn their preparation. He insisted, so I said, "Well, maybe just a little". The meal consisted of a Turkish salad with tomatoes, cucumber slices, onions, olives, and cheese mixed in olive oil. My plate was handed to me with a large scoop of fried rice with green specks in it and two cups of brown beans. I hate brown beans ordinarily but these were seasoned very well and were tasty. There wasn't any meat with the meal. They haven't eaten meat in the past 15 years; they eat only fish and chicken. It's no wonder that most Turks are lean and slim.

Waiting for my crewmember to show up was boring. He called Wednesday to say that he was being delayed by his job as a ski instructor and bus driver. He said that he was going to try to make it by next Monday. I tried to stay busy. I refinished the companionway doors using a heat gun, scraper and sander borrowed from Videt. I did a lot of swimming and walking. I slept in the afternoons and rowed to shore around 5:00 p.m. to sit in the shade and sip tea with the boatyard workers and the fishermen. Yesterday we ate a large watermelon. One day I helped Captain Evart untangle the lines to his mooring. We tied a water jug on the lines to make it easier to pick them up.

I spent most of Wednesday on anchor watch as the wind veered to the northwest and picked up to 30 knots. There were considerable waves rounding the mountain shore and hitting "Idyllic" broadside, rolling her and yanking on the mooring line. I read Patrick O'Brian's book, "Blue at the Mizzen", to pass the time more quickly. I wanted to go to town for a beer and some belly dancing, but the wind kept me boat bound.

Thursday I went to both bazaars; the one bazaar for hard supplies, tools, clothes, and towels; the other bazaar for vegetables, a chicken, a duck, spices, cheese, bread, and olives. Figure 27 is a picture of a spice booth in the marketplace. I bought a week's supply of food for $10 USD. There was a large crowd of buyers and sellers. Tea was offered to one and all. It was fun and very exciting with lots of noise. On the way back in the dinghy, the waves had built up and I got thoroughly soaked

On Friday, I watched a new, 75-ton fishing boat, "Ahmet", being launched. He put his anchor right over the top of mine. I hoped he would leave before I did, so I wouldn't have a problem getting my line up. A sheep was killed as a sacrifice in their traditional celebration of the launching. There was a party with food and all of the trimmings. I talked to William, the Frenchman, and Roger, the Englishman, for the rest of the morning. I sold copies of my first two books to them. I took the dolmus to Bodrum in the afternoon to buy camping gaz (butane) and some chain for the anchor rode at Bodrum Hardware where I was invited to have tea.

The next day I helped William launch his boat "Mawi". He had added an electric starter to avoid the usual hand cranking and put in wheel steering. The fishermen steer a tiller with their foot while standing up to see over the cabin. This was the only one that I had seen so modernized. Figure 28 is a picture of a typical small fishing boat.

Saturday, Bryan Stephens, the English hotel owner in Yalikavak, invited me to sail on his boat, "Funda". This boat, shown in Figure 29, is an old Turkish gullet made entirely of pinewood. It is immaculately maintained and the love of his life. Sunday, Bryan and I were joined by Bryan's charming Turkish wife Olcay, Bryan's teenage son, and a newly wed couple. Bryan, his wife, and son are shown aboard in Figure 30. The "honeymoon"couple is shown in Figure 31. We left the harbor without much wind and sailed south to Gumusluk where we tied up to the village pier for 10M TL. It was a hot day, so three of us went for a swim. This was followed by a meal that Olcay had prepared in advance. The meal consisted of a type of Turkish pizza that was very flavorful and filling. Figure 32 shows Gumusluk Harbor.

Bryan's boat, "Funda", sailed beautifully and tracked very well but she turned and backed with some difficulty due to her full keel.

Figure 27
Spice booth

Figure 28
Fishing boat

Figure 29
Roger's boat, "Funda"

Figure 33 shows "Funda" sailing. We had trouble reversing and backing up to the pier (Mediterranean style docking), especially after letting go the anchor too soon and running out of anchor chain while backing up to the pier. We had to retrieve the anchor and start over. This was a slow process with the old anchor windlass and gave the shore-side captains and tourists entertainment for quite some time. We attracted the village policeman to catch our dock lines when we finally neared the pier. The newly wed couple was interested in each other and not much help during the sailing and docking. However, Bryan's wife and son were experienced and everything went fairly smoothly. Figure 34 is a picture of me at the helm.

At the end of the month of June, my new crewmember, Etienne De Bruyne, finally showed up a month late and I was able to leave Yalikavak for my summer sail.

Figure 30
Bryan, his wife, and his son

Figure 31
Honeymoon couple

Figure 32
Gumusluk Harbor

Figure 33
"Funda" sailing

Figure 34

Harold Knoll at the helm of "Funda"

Yalikavak, Turkey to Istanbul, Turkey

On Friday, July 2nd, we finally left Yalikavak sailing against the prevailing north winds. We had been held up for three days of Meltemi storm. Out at sea in good-sized waves, our steering cable broke. I immediately broke out the emergency steering tiller that had been buried under 14 year's accumulation of equipment. After bolting it on, it worked fairly well, but made me appreciate my wheel steering that I had long been taking for granted. We sailed all the way to Yero Kambos Harbor on Leros Island, Greece. This was far west of our desired course, but we hoped we would have a better course off the wind to get north from Leros Island. While we were there, I tried to dismantle the steering column but the bolts were too tight for my tools so we planned to sail to Port Lakki the next day to hire a mechanic to help fix the steering.

Yero Kambos Harbor was incredibly scenic. To the south were the rugged mountains of Kilminos shining in the setting sun, stark without trees and with very little greenery. To the east was a craggy mountain with a conglomeration of goats, pigeons, and dog cages on its side. I saw a man carrying bags of food and pails of water for his animals that were all following him up the steep mountainside as if he were the Pied Piper. Even a flock of pigeons was flying around his head waiting for food and attention. To the west was a small village with the ubiquitous whitewashed, box-style houses with blue trim all covered with bougainvillea. The chug of the fishing boats, the whine of wind in the rigging, and the ringing of the goat bells on the mountainside sounded like some large orchestra. To the north there were more mountains terraced and walled in stone by ancient farmers. In the valley between the mountains lay the small village with its palm nut and fruit trees. Perfume was drifting over the bay from the bougainvillea and oleander blossoms. All of this made for a very pleasant evening after a trying day at sea.

Saturday we sailed seven miles to Port Lakki. On the way, we lost our anchor overboard. I was just going below for a cup of tea when I heard the rattle of chain over the anchor rollers. I immediately worked my way forward in high seas to stop it from running out, but most of the rode was already out. When we had been coming into our last port, I had untied the anchor in preparation for anchoring. We picked up a buoy instead, didn't use the anchor, and I forgot to tie it back down.

For the next several miles, I sat on the bow and paid for my mistake by riding up and crashing down while pulling on the chain with all of my strength to recover short lengths each time we descended down from the top of a wave. Soaked in spray, I pulled almost all the way to Port Lakki and finally won the battle.

Sailing into the bay, I found the Evros Marina boat yard with a small quay where we tied up. The next morning I walked into the boatyard and met Bob, the mechanic and all-around maintenance man. I explained the problem and he immediately left to get a new cable. He found a halyard cable and went to work dismantling the pedestal. We worked together in the rising hot sun and two hours later we were finished. This cost me 130 EU, which included our stay at the quay for the night. Later we walked to town and had a delicious Musaka dinner.

On July 4th, Independence Day, we sailed northwest against a lively north wind. It was a beautiful, clear day and everything was working right, including the new steering cable. We traveled 36 miles but only made 6 miles on our course north. We anchored in Kambos Bay, Patmos Island, Greece. Soon after anchoring, we started dragging, so I pulled the anchor and motored in closer to shore. Once again the steering cable broke. I quickly dropped the anchor and started looking for the problem. This time I was intimately familiar with the mechanism and diagnosed the problem right away. The clamps on the cable had come loose. Bob either had not properly tightened them or they were too large for the cable. I spent the rest of the evening reattaching them.

During the night, there was a lot of gunfire at the restaurant on the beach and we wondered if a war was starting. There was also a lot of cheering and blowing of car horns. Later, we learned that Greece had won the futbal finals against Portugal. The next morning, we woke up early after a fitful night's sleep due to the high winds to find even higher winds that kept us in port all day.

Being trapped in port, we took the bus to the town of Skala to sightsee. Ferryboats and cruise ships bring many tourists to the island of Patmos so we had lots of company wherever we went. The harbor is ringed with docks and there are yachts and fishing boats all around. I purchased a Greek T-shirt for 7 EU. I bought two loaves of bread and then we took the bus back to the anchorage at Kambos. Etienne and I went to the local restaurant on the beach and each ate a very delicious stuffed tomato accompanied by a Stella Artois beer.

On the way back to the beach, we had to clamber over some large boulders to reach our dinghy that we had hidden on the craggy shore. When Etienne attempted to climb over one of the boulders, he twisted his knee and fell back onto the rocky shore. It was very painful and I was afraid that it was broken, but Etienne insisted that it wasn't. The next morning it had swollen and was very painful. I put Ace bandages around it and gave him Ibuprofen and Vicodin. Greece has a high rate of accidents. My crewmember, Larry Sharp, and his scooter were victims last year.

Leaving port and sailing the bounding main is difficult for somebody who has difficulty standing. High winds and waves continued for the next two days and kept us in port.

I spent the morning of July 7th washing some clothes in a 3-gallon bucket with a toilet plunger. I washed in salt water and rinsed in fresh water. We played some cards and I tried to get my computer going again. It had become necessary to write my notes longhand.

Overlooking the harbor of Patmos is the Monastery of St. John and the town of Chora on top of the mountain. Nearby is the cave where St. John composed the book of Revelations for the Bible. The cave is now a pilgrimage site for the faithful and the tourists arrive by the busloads.

I went to work on the steering cables again. I bought new smaller size cable clamps that fit the cable better and should hold. I also tightened the tension adjustment to make the helm more responsive to the touch. I cooked dinner and Etienne, trying to be diplomatic, called my culinary masterpiece, "Very colorful".

For seven days now the Meltemi had blown straight out of the north. We were unable to move outside the protection of the island of Patmos. It was boring, frustrating, and worrisome that we were using up valuable time sitting in port. This bad weather had thrown my schedule way off. I was supposed to be in Istanbul by the 18th and it was still 500 miles away.

I decided to see the Monastery of St. John. Etienne had already visited it so I went alone. I took the dinghy to shore and picked up a dolmus to travel over the mountains to Skala. Ferries, yachts, and fishing boats all use the port of Skala. On the shore there are restaurants, souvenir shops, gift shops, supermarkets, shipping agencies, and a small beach. From Skala I took a late bus to Chora, which is an ancient city that shares the mountaintop with the Monastery of St. John. On top, there is a panoramic view of Ikara and Samos Islands to the north as shown in Figure 35. Chora is a Byzantine city with the Byzantine cross on many old buildings situated on very old, narrow, crooked streets. Some streets were constructed only a few feet wide to discourage pirate attacks and to confuse and frustrate marauding invaders.

On the side of the mountain is the cave of the Apocalypse where St. John saw a vision and dictated the Book of Revelations. The Monastery itself looks like a fairy castle. It was built to withstand attack from the sides and preserve the treasury of over 200 ancient icons, 300 pieces of silver and gold, and dazzling jewels. It is one of the most important places of worship among Orthodox Christians. The main entryway has high slots above it to be used for pouring boiling oil on attackers or uninvited guests. Entry to the monastery is free, but with a 6 EU charge to see the treasury. Figures 36 through 41 show the Monastery.

On July 10th, we finally got away from Patmos and sailed northeast to Pithagorio Harbor on Samos Island and spent the night there. The next day, we started out of Pithagorio harbor and got hit by high wind and waves before we even got out of the shelter of the two mountains on the island and the Turkish mainland. We needed to sail a course of 30 degrees to reach our destination but could only make good a course of 70 degrees. The waves were considerable and soon the spray was flying. "Idyllic" was bouncing like a crazy horse and it was necessary to turn back and anchor in the bay again. The attempt out to sea and back was 7 miles in length.

The next day we were able to reach the port of Kusadasi on the Turkish coast where there was a modern city marina. After registering and paying an exorbitant mooring fee, I went exploring. Etienne was not up to much exploring because of his injured knee. After buying some groceries and

Figure 35
View from top of Monastery

Figure 36
Entrance to Monastery

Figure 37
Inside the Monastery

Figure 38
Bells on top of the Monastery

Figure 39
Priest lighting candles

Figure 40
Icon in Monastery

Figure 41
Two Orthodox Priests

small supplies, I looked around a bit before returning to "Idyllic" and my bunk.

After getting directions from the shopkeepers, we easily found the bus station, which had buses to Ephesus (Effes) every 20 minutes. Effes is also the name of the most popular Turkish beer and the name of the two guard dogs back at the Tokar boatyard. A taxi driver offered to give us a round trip to Ephesus for 50M TL. He also offered some interesting tips on visiting Ephesus. He said that it was about 15 kilometers to the entrance but if we took the dolmus, we would have to walk 2 kilometers from the bus stop to the entrance. We took the dolmus to the bus stop where there was a side road to Effes. After walking the two kilometers, we came to the main parking lot at the entrance to the city. There were restaurants, souvenir shops, and public baths at this entrance.

Ephesus is an ancient Hellenistic city with later Roman ruins overlaying it. It was the capital of the province and the center of arts, commerce, worship, and government. The city was founded about 1000 BC and has been occupied by Lydians, Cairns, Romans and Goths. At various times the citizens worshiped a number of different gods there. The temple of Artemis was one of the seven wonders of the ancient world. Walking down the marble roads shown in Figure 42, we met hordes of tourists from the three cruise ships in the harbor of Kusadasi. One of the ships was the "Princess". We saw the theater, a beautiful library shown in Figure 43, the Agora Stadium shown in Figure 44, a gymnasium, and a brothel. We learned about the evolution of religious belief from the many gods of the time on into the Christian era when monotheism replaced polytheism. Figure 45 shows a community toilet and Figure 46 shows some tourist women trying it for size.

Nearby was the Hagia Maria where Mary, mother of Jesus, lay after her death. The Acts of the Apostles and the letters to Ephesus were sent there. St. Paul preached there in 53 A.D. Eventually the river and the harbor silted up shutting down the sea commerce. Later, several earthquakes shook the city into total destruction.

The city of Ephesus was very impressive. The citizens had beautiful homes with hot and cold running water, sewers, fountains, baths, theaters, a vast library, a large arena, and paved roads. One emperor, who had conquered the known world, had a statue of himself carved with his foot on a round world. 1400 years later in Western Europe, people were put to death who dared speculate about the world being round.

After seeing the ancient city, I took a dolmus to Selcuk to see the Ephesus Museum, which was very educational. I found the historical display of gladiators to be especially moving. Many statues and artifacts that had been found by archeologists were on display and many of them

Figure 42
Marble roads in Ephesus

Figure 43
Theater in Ephesus

Figure 44
Library building in Ephesus

were perfectly preserved.

As I was waiting for the museum to open, I heard a band playing. Being always attracted to music, I sauntered over to investigate and saw a parade coming. First there was a priest dressed in a white gown with splendid gold trim, carrying a Turkish flag. Next came two clerics carrying colorful flags that I presumed to be religious. These were followed by four more clerics carrying additional colorful flags. Next in line was what appeared to be a very beautiful young girl dressed in an elaborate white wedding dress that was the most beautiful I had ever seen. She was riding high up on the very top of a horse drawn carriage. A band followed playing unusual music with horns and drums. This music was different from any that I had ever heard. Then came cars and a truck all overflowing with men, women, and children all dressed in their best clothes. The one thing missing was the groom. I inquired about this in a nearby teahouse. The explanation was

Figure 45
Toilets in Ephesus

Figure 46
Ladies trying out toilet seats

long and elaborate, and I understood very little of it since it was in Turkish. Finally a kind young girl explained to me that this was not a wedding but a circumcision celebration. The "bride" was a 13-year-old boy. His very rich parents had sponsored the elaborate decorations and large parade.

Later, walking back to meet Etienne, I saw two storks standing on their large nest on top of a concrete power pole. Further on, I saw two more flying about in the most graceful manner, like an airplane with a very large wingspan. It had been a wonderful day.

On Monday we motor sailed 50 miles north from Kusadasi up the coast of Turkey and anchored in a bay called Zeytinelli Korfez. This was a quaint Rest and Recuperation facility for Turkish Air Force personnel. Chow time was announced by bugle and we were tempted to join them, as we were hungry. Figure 47 shows the coast of Turkey.

Tuesday we sailed with an unusual south wind, which is almost

Figure 47
Northern Aegean coast of Turkey

43

unheard of in these waters. We went up the strait between the Turkish mainland and the Island of Nisos Lypso, Greece, at 6 mph with the wind on the stern quarter at 30 knots. The waves were small at first but building all day. About evening time, a storm appeared to be brewing with black rain clouds threatening but no rain came. We sailed into the ancient port of Foca, where there was a crowd of Turkish tourists. There were many families with young people taking rides in horse carriages and walking the promenade around the harbor. I treated Etienne to a beer and he bought me an ice-cream cone.

The next day we left Foca vowing to return some day. We got a late start as the Harbor Master had locked the electric service box with our cable connection inside. He finally showed up with the key to our box but not the neighbor's box. They had wanted to leave also. We motor sailed out against very rough seas. We had 20 knot winds dead against us all the way up the coast of Nisos Lesvos Island with Etienne at the helm doing an excellent job of handling the boat in the adverse conditions. The sun continued to be very hot.

We finally came to a large fiord on Lesvos Island. We went up the fiord and anchored in a large protected bay called Kolpas Kalloni. We were near the quaint fishing village of Apothekes. As we motored into the entrance to the bay, a fisherman yelled something in Greek. Simultaneously, I noticed the depth was up to only a little over 5 feet. I quickly understood his urgent warning and turned just in time to avoid a reef, thanks to an unknown friend, a Greek fisherman.

On Thursday, July 15th, we sailed all day around the big island of Nisos Lesvos in large waves and 30-knot winds tacking 67 miles between 6:30 a.m. and 7:00 p.m. but gaining only a little mileage northward on our course. I had wanted to go the other way around the island through the strait, which would have been protected. Etienne thought that we could save 20 miles on our course the way we went. Instead, we lost 30 miles on the course and wasted a whole day. Etienne said that he doesn't understand my curious (meaning dumb) way of thinking. We finished the day in Sivrice, Turkey. One day we're in Turkey and the next day illegally in Greece and then back in Turkey again the next day. Maybe we should try smuggling.

The next day we left at dawn to beat the daily rising winds, but a meltemi caught up with us full force at about 10:00 a.m. It blew so hard that 17 freighters anchored in the protection of Bozcaada Island to wait for better conditions. The "Idyllic" struggled on through the wind and waves with the spray flying, as was everything in the cabin that wasn't tied down. We tacked upwind for 45 miles to cover 20 or less on course. Sailing into the harbor out of the windstorm, we found Bozcaada to be truly a haven

Figure 48
Bozcaada Castle

Figure 49
Bozcaada Castle

of peace. Bozcaada is a military base and a prime tourist island with a beautiful fortress guarding the harbor and the strategic entrance to the Dardanelle Straits. Figures 48 and 49 are pictures of the Bozcaada Castle. When I walked around town, I needed a light jacket for the first time this summer. The temperature was dropping slowly as we traveled north.

A Belidse (city officer) showed up to collect the dock fee and warn us that we were tied up the wrong way (bow instead of stern to the dock).

Figure 50
Tanker entering the Dardanelle

Allowing him to keep an extra 500,000 TL with the fee convinced him that it would be OK this time. The meltemi, with Beaufort 5-6, was predicted again for the next day when we would be traveling through the Dardanelles. We were only 15 miles from the entrance to the straits.

We left the harbor at 6:00 a.m. in order to try to get into the Dardanelles Strait before the meltemi had time to build up the wind and waves in the open sea. We attempted to sail but the large freighters passing in a steady stream in the narrow entrance forced us to motor most of the way. This strait is a virtual freeway for many different kinds of ships from all over the world. Figure 50 is a picture of a tanker entering the Dardanelles.

On the north side of the entrance to the strait, there is a monument to the fallen British soldiers of World War I. Further up, across the strait from Canakkle, there is a monument on the north side to the fallen Turkish soldiers of World War I. We finally arrived at the harbor in Canakkle, which is right in the middle of the town. Canakkle was founded when the harbor of ancient Troy, located a little further south, finally silted up about 500 AD. A Turkish Coast Guard (Sahil Guvenlik) boat, manned by four men armed with machineguns, showed up there immediately to check our papers. For the first time in my sailing trip, I encountered two Russian and two Belgium sailboats in a Turkish harbor.

The next day, Sunday, July 18, we left early and sailed 30 miles through the strait against a 5-knot current. Some boats were unable to move against the current. There were towboats available to them for a very steep price. We stopped at the town of Gelibolu, a ferry port on the north side of the Dardanelles at the entrance to the Sea of Marmara. We anchored in 6 meters of water with a good-holding sand bottom, as it appeared that there wasn't any room in the small, crowded, commercial harbor.

We watched tugboats, ferries, cargo vessels, and fishing boats go in and out of the harbor in a steady stream. We went swimming with a lot of jellyfish around; they seemed harmless but were a little disconcerting. In the evening, we saw two Turkish wedding receptions. There was some slow but graceful dancing by the women only. The reception line consisted of men and women kissing the cheeks of the bride and groom. The oldest female well-wishers also received a kiss on the hand and lifted their hand to their forehead. There were well over 400 people in attendance. I feel fortunate to have witnessed, at different times, a Greek Orthodox funeral, a circumcision parade, and a Turkish wedding celebration.

In Turkey, many cafés have water pipes (narghiles) with several mouthpiece connections for patrons to smoke. The older Turks use them on a regular basis and some tourists try them. Contrary to popular belief, they had only tobacco in them. Hashish is forbidden by law. All drugs are forbidden and the penalties for violation are very severe.

On Monday, we arose at 4:00 a.m. and found the wind to be moderate. We motored 12 miles up the coast straight into the prevailing northeast wind before the fuel filter plugged up and the engine quit. Etienne turned "Idyllic" downwind and kept her steady to give me a chance to work, upside down through the engine hatch, on the two fuel filters. One was on the hull side and the other on the fuel pump at the engine. I replaced both filters, which was not an easy job, bouncing around on a rough sea. The screen on the fuel pump filter was full of brown gunk. After the cleaning, the engine started easily, but by that time the waves had gotten tremendously high forcing us to retreat all the way back to Gelibolu. We tied up at the commercial quay behind a large red freighter for protection. Cargo boats and ferries were coming in and out all night rocking the boat and making sleep difficult.

The next day was another miserable day of motoring against the wind and high waves. I was getting very tired of the bad weather, fighting each day to make a few miles. I was already several days behind schedule getting to Istanbul to meet Bassem, my next crewmember. We arrived in Sarkoy harbor at 2:00 p.m., tired and frustrated. Sarkoy is a fishing harbor operated by the fishermen. The fish restaurant on the dock takes care of the few yachts that visit. I cleaned a lot of gunk out of the filters again. The engine was running hot, so I replaced the Johnson water pump impeller. These were two projects that were not high on my list of enjoyable things to do. I dislike mechanical work but dislike paying a mechanic even more, so I do the work myself.

The marina clubhouse set says that there are usually 3 to 6 days of meltemi followed by a day of calm and then the prevailing wind. However, we have just had 6 straight days of meltemi with more predicted. We continued to slog up the coast of the Marmara Sea noticing more and more development along the shore. The shore was covered with large developments having row after row of Turkish style concrete box houses.

As we approached Istanbul, we were greeted by the awful stench of sewage. The Turks pipe their sewage out to sea causing massive pollution. Yet, there were thousands of Istanbul citizens along the shore enjoying the beachfront and frolicking in the sea. The sea was literally brown and I cringed at the spray being thrown onto the deck and in our faces. Fortunately, the rest of our stay here was much more pleasant. Figure 51 is a picture of Istanbul from the Marmara Sea.

We entered the Atakoy Marina and tied up at one of their docks. I immediately started trying to locate Bassem who had been waiting for me since July 18th, almost a week! First I asked at the marina office and was told that they had not heard from him. Soon after, the Port Control Officer came to the "Idyllic" and reported that Bassem had been looking for me and was staying at the nearby Holiday Inn. Checking at the Inn, I discovered that the room had been too expensive and he had left without a forwarding address. I called home to see if my wife had heard from him and found that he had left a number where he could be reached at the Sultan Hostel. I called there and found that he was out. I left a message with my location and a promise to call back. Back at the boat, the marina control tower called me to say that Bassem was looking for me. Next, a security officer came to the boat to tell me that Bassem was on the phone at the reception office. I went to the office and we talked on the phone, making arrangements to meet the next day at 11:00 a.m. Bassem wanted to know if I would be up by then. I assured him that I was up by 6:00 a.m. every day! Figure 52 is a picture of Bassem and Etienne talking in the cabin of the "Idyllic". Figure 53 shows the route that "Idyllic" took from Yalikavak to Istanbul.

Figure 51
Istanbul, Turkey

Figure 52
Bassem and Etienne

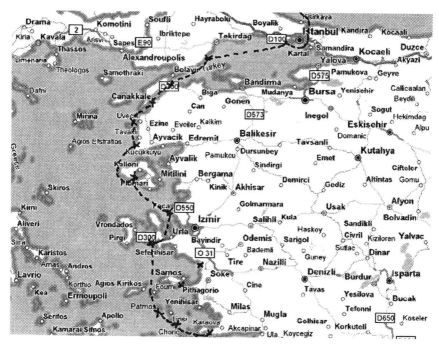

Figure 53
Route from Yalikavak to Istanbul

Istanbul, Turkey to Varna, Bulgaria

On July 24th when preparing to leave Turkey, I read in the Cruising Guide that Karakoy was the last place to clear out of Turkey going north. I found Karakoy on the map and then asked directions at the Marina Reception. They informed me that I should take green bus #81. Thus began an all day trek via bus, walking, and taxi that eventually consumed seven hours of time and 50 kilometers of travel.

First to the Port Police, then two kilometers over the Galata Bridge spanning the Golden Horn, and then up the waterfront to be told that we needed the Harbor Masters stamp first, which was one kilometer farther on. We walked three kilometers before we arrived at the Bureau where we obtained his stamp of approval. Then we returned three kilometers to Customs for their stamp. Then all we had to do was go to the Zeaport (seaport) for the Passport Police approval, stamp and signature.

Bassem was completely worn out by this time and frustrated. He had not experienced such bureaucracy before. He gave up, handed me his passport, and promised to see me back at the boat. Bassem had a Jordanian Passport and this caused the Passport Police considerable concern. They did a lot of phone calling and made a minute inspection of the passport. They finally opened a briefcase stuffed with different forms and stamps. Then, with great formality, they stamped the passports and ship's papers and told me to have a nice day. My day and my patience were already gone. Then they told me that I had to submit four copies of these documents!

They told me that the marina would make the copies for me, but while I was waiting for the bus I saw a Volvo dealership. I went in and asked them if they could make four copies for me and they did. I immediately went back up the street to the Passport Control office and handed in the copies to a very surprised control officer. After a five-kilometer bus ride, I reported to the Marina Reception secretary who was also surprised to see me back so soon. She shook my hand and congratulated me over and over. That night Bassem came back too tired to join me for a Turkish dinner in the city. I had beef kabob that was very spicy.

The next day, Sunday, we left the Atakoy Marina at 7:00 a.m. after three days of hectic preparations during which I really didn't have time to see much of Istanbul. We had to motor against a 3-4 knot current and play games with the eddies by going inside of bays, back of points, and crossing to avoid the fastest currents. Dodging the large freighters took constant attention, since they cannot stop or turn to avoid a boat and one miscalculation or bit of inattention might be your last.

We finally arrived at the port of Poyazkoy, which is at the northern end of the Bosphorus Strait. There were about 100 boats anchored in the small harbor. This harbor is shown in Figure 54. The beach was full of tourists and we donned our swimsuits and joined the crowd swimming in the Black sea. This water is not as salty as the Mediterranean Sea and we had to paddle more to stay afloat. The water here in the mouth of the Bosphorus was blue and not black like the Black Sea. The Black Sea was once called the Pontus Euxinnus (the Hospital Sea) because of the minerals it contained.

Bassem met a young lady while swimming and soon two Turks swam out and invited him to shore for a bier (beer). The whole family was there to greet him and ply him with questions while the young lady translated. He thoroughly enjoyed the attention and hospitality.

The coast of Turkey northwest from the Bosphorus has very few ports to take refuge in if a storm should come. The nearest is Cilingos Koyu,

Figure 54
Poyazkoy Harbor and beach

which is 45 miles up the coast. These shores are low lying and laced with open-pit brown coal mines. There are only a few villages and resorts. These resorts have nice sand beaches.

I was still having difficulties with fuel contamination. I had evidently gotten some dirty fuel and I had to clean the gunk out of the fuel filters again and again. I was running out of filters and needed some more. I was hoping that my next crewmember, Harold Byler, could bring some from the States.

We next anchored in the beautiful small bay just off the large sand beach at Cilingos. There were only a few cottages and house trailers along the road. There was almost total silence there. We had sailed for almost 50 miles without seeing a single boat of any kind: not a rowboat, a sailboat, a fishing boat, or a freighter.

The bay was filled with unusual looking jellyfish. At first Bassem only followed me through the water. Later, he gained confidence and swam wearing a life preserver all the way to shore. The Coast Guard (Sahil Guvenlik) boats in Turkey are numerous and very well equipped. They met Bassem as he swam to shore, perhaps thinking that he was an illegal alien. On the way back, the life preserver disintegrated and a Coast Guardsman picked him up to keep him from drowning and gave him a ride back to the boat.

We spent a miserable night in the exposed harbor rocking to the swell of the Black Sea. It was 1:00 a.m. before I finally drifted off to sleep. Everything that was loose was rolling, knocking, clinking, banging, squeaking, or making some other objectionable sound. I tried out the bunk, the wet cockpit, the cabin roof, the dinghy, and finally the cabin sole, which was the lowest and most stable place on the boat.

The next day while sailing, the topping lift cable broke where it had been tangled with the radar reflector. This required me to climb the mast to reattach it. We ended the day in Igneada Harbor where the Coast Guard motioned for us to go away from the quay, even though the Cruising Guide said that we could tie up there. They pointed to the fishing dock but, when we went there, it was full. We finally anchored in three meters of water with a good mud bottom and 360 degrees of shelter.

The weather here seemed to be different every day. One day it was hazy and cloudy all over the horizon. The day before it was sun with patches of high clouds. The day before that had bright sun all day. Each day began with a land breeze and then changed direction around 10:00 a.m. to a sea breeze of less than 10 knots.

I had one problem that I had not yet solved: how to get to Bulgaria. The Cruising Guide says that the only port of entry is Burgas, which is far north on the coast. If we sailed all the way to Burgas, we would miss seeing most of Bulgaria. Etienne, as well as my other friends in Yalika-vak, made sure that I knew how bad the Bulgarians are! They assured me that it is not safe to go there. "The country is full of thieves and bandits. Those people from the East are terrible." In my past travels, I have been told the same thing about the Spanish, French, Germans, etc. It's really amazing how widespread this fear of strangers is.

On Wednesday, we took the dinghy to shore and headed out on foot to visit the town of Igneada that is about 5 km from the harbor. Bassem wanted to take a taxi but the driver wanted 15 Euro, which was too much. We hitchhiked and caught a ride on a tractor-pulled lumber wagon. Several lumbermen were in the wagon, which had high posts on the sides to hold the logs. We literally flew, hanging on for dear life, over the bumpy, crooked road. There were 30 or 40 more lumber wagons sitting around the town. I gave the driver the Coke that I had purchased for my walk to town. In town, we saw the Turkish Post Office (PTT), bought some groceries, and went swimming at the town beach.

On the way back to the boat, we caught a ride on a food delivery truck that dropped us off half way back. There we found an Internet Café but their computer would only send our outgoing messages and not read our incoming messages. When we got back to the dinghy, we found that somebody had thrown dead fish into it. This was probably the taxi driver and was certainly not a very friendly gesture. Figure 55 shows Bassem playing Bache (Backgammon) with a local fisherman.

On Thusday, we went to sea early. The wind was moderate but the waves were 10 feet. We did not want to fight those waves for 50 miles, so we returned to Igneada and tied up at an empty space at the fishing pier. We went back to the Internet Café but their computer had crashed completely this time. We went swimming but the water was full of green,

Figure 55
Bassem playing backgammon

floating scum and weeds. We collected some mussels and cooked them for dinner along with some small fish we bought that looked like mackerel. The fish seller agreed to take us by car to Burgas, Bulgaria, at 6:00 a.m. the next morning. This would allow us to get some Bulgarian money, a visa, and a cruising permit. I was very happy to get this opportunity.

The next morning the fish seller had changed his mind. He claimed that a shipment of fish was coming from Istanbul. This was a setback for our plans and a big disappointment for me. That evening, the weather looked good with west winds and calm seas, so we left at 3:30 a.m. the next morning. We started off motor sailing but at 5:00a.m., we picked up a plastic sheet on the propeller and had to turn the engine off. We sailed until 8:00 a.m. I dove down and, after several repeated tries in big waves, cut the plastic off. "Idyllic" kept crashing down on my head making my underwater work difficult and dangerous. We then sailed all the way to

Burgas where we were boarded by the Port Police, along with Customs and Immigration, at their commercial dock. We did not encounter any problems other than the usual frustrating paperwork and stupid questions like. "Do you have any illegal aliens on board?" I looked under the table and said, "No, no aliens on board." He frowned. I guess that he didn't have much sense of humor. They took our passports and the ship's papers for safekeeping and had us move to the tugboat quay where we had to stay until Monday when we got our Bulgarian Cruising Permit.

In spite of all of the previous warnings by Etienne about the evil people of the East, the Bulgarians were friendly, helpful, and cooperative. I walked the dark streets at night without incident. The Burgas residents didn't beg, harass, or bother me in any way; however, they were not overly friendly. There weren't any greetings unless I said hello and started a conversation. I'm always amazed by how Europeans mistrust each other, probably as a result of the years of European warfare. I found the prices in Bulgaria to be very cheap for just about everything.

Monday morning, I checked in with the authorities at 6:45 a.m. and was told that I needed to visit the Harbor Master's Office later after they opened. In the meantime, I arranged for the fuel truck to come at 8:00 a.m. When the driver, Larry, showed up, he put in 156 liters of diesel fuel for 195 lev (BGL), which is about $129 USD. Fuel is cheap in this part of the world. Afterwards, I climbed six floors of a building to discover that I had been given the wrong location for the Harbor Master's Office and needed to go to a different building two kilometers away. When I arrived there, I spent an hour with six officials and a very charming lady with a perfectly arranged desk After several phone calls, they told me to go back to the Harbor Master's Office in the other building. I was personally escorted by an underling who did not say a single word the entire trip.

However, he did make sure that I didn't get away. This time we found the correct office on the fourth floor. This office had three officers that were operating computers. They asked for the Owner's Certificate, our passports, and the Port Police Report. I gave them this information and then they wanted to know how long I needed a permit for.

After carefully trying to read the US Treasury Certification, they asked for an explanation. They wanted to know how many meters is 32 feet and why, if I lived in Montague, Michigan, the Certificate said Chicago. Then they said that it would take an hour to fill in the permit and that I should come back later for the permit. I went back down the four flights of stairs and across the street where I purchased an orange juice for 1.5 lev. I sat back and watched the locals, loaded down with baskets of supplies, walk past to the beach for a day of fun.

After an hour of relaxation, I climbed back up the stairs to the office to be met by a problem. My registration papers were out of date and had expired in November of 2003. I assured them that the registration was up to date and they told me to prove it. I raised my voice and protested to no avail. I argued and pleaded in my most persuasive voice with my arms flapping like I learned in Italy, but they had heard it all before. We finally agreed that I would e-mail the US Treasury and obtain a fax verifying the registration. When I was replacing my papers, I found the latest certification in an envelope lost in the back of the folder. The entire office broke out in laughter. They were as relieved as I was. About this time, God took a hand and turned off all the electricity so that all of the computers went down. It was out of everybody's hands. I waited around drinking coffee with the brass in their pure white uniforms. Captain Zhelyo Valkon did the translating. His position was Senior Inspection Flag State Control, Port of Burgas. He entertained me until the electricity came back on.

Soon after, a Temporary Navigation Certificate was signed, stamped, and issued to me. Figure 56 is a copy of that Certificate and Figure 57 is a copy of the regulations accompanying the Certificate. Afterward, we remained tied up to the tugboat quay on the edge of the downtown area and nobody said anything. The yacht marina is around the north side of the bay about two kilometers from downtown and not very convenient at all.

After a great mackerel dinner that night, I met a very interesting character. He is Captain Jonathan (Jon) Olsen from New Zealand. His boat is an older, wooden, 60-foot former racing sailboat. It has a beam of only 11 feet and a single, very tall mast. This boat, with a full keel, is very difficult to handle in some of the small harbors. After we had a few beers, he told me the story of his arrival in the small harbor at Canakkale, Turkey, with a 40km wind blowing. Discovering that the gearshift lever was jammed, he quickly sent a crewmember, Mart, down below to do the shifting manually. When Jon called down for a shift, Mart was required to reach around a hot exhaust pipe to operate a small lever that shifted the gears. This resulted in a significant delay between the orders and the actual shifting.

In the harbor, not knowing that there were mooring lines attached to the quay, Jon planned to drop the anchor off the stern as he went in, bow first, to the quay. They went in too fast downwind and an overeager crewmember dropped the anchor and secured it much too soon. This stopped the boat short of the quay and the waiting dock master. With Jon yelling "Forward" and "Reverse", Mart shifting furiously down below, several observers and the dock master yelling instructions from different viewpoints in a strange language, things went badly. At one point, the Harbor Master jumped aboard from another boat that Jon had crashed into. He was yelling, "You crazy captain!" The entire episode was a

REPUBLIC OF BULGARIA
MINISTRY OF TRANSPORT AND COMMUNICATION
MARITIME ADMINISTRATION OF BULGARIA

TEMPORARY NAVIGATION
CERTIFICATE

THE MARITIME ADMINISTRATION of BULGARIA certifies that,

s/v "IDYLLIC" owners: HAROLD KNOLL JR, 600 FRUITVALE RD, MONTAGUE, MI 49437 flag, register UNITED STATES OF AMERICA No 1074257 IMO № CPY00276K788 , with valid ship's documents is temporary registered in port of BURGAS Reg. No 7/TR Book under the command of Capt. Harold Knoll Jr

It is permitted to sail in the territorial waters of the Republic of Bulgaria till five nautical miles off shore, up to 4 Beaford scale in daytime and visit the following areas and ports:

All Bulgarian Black sea ports

Valid until: 09.08. 04

Date of issue: 02.08.2004
Place of issue: BURGAS

No . 17851

DIRECTOR, MARITIME
ADMINISTRATION -Burgas

(Capt. V. Ivanov)

REMARK: The holder of the present Certificate to follow strictly the Bulgarian Maritime Regulations and laws and to return it to Harbour Master's representatives before leaving the country.

Figure 56
Bulgarian Temporary Navigation Certificate

disaster. This brings to mind an old saying, "If in doubt, run in circles, scream and shout!" The whole scenario sounded even more exciting after a few beers late at night at a sidewalk café in Burgas, Bulgaria.

The next morning Jon's cook, Vickie, told me that his billfold, with credit cards, had been stolen by two young ladies of the night. He spent the next few days e-mailing credit card companies.

From Burgas, we sailed to Bayla and anchored in the harbor, as there wasn't anyone to help dock and we didn't know which moorings were

REGULATIONS

For skippers and foreign yachts' crews obligations, supplied with the Temporary Navigation Certificate

1. An incoming and outgoing control of the yachts and its crew to be done in Port Varna only.

2. The yacht is permitted to visit only the following ports :Balchik , ~~Obzor~~, Burgas , Sozopol, Pomorie, Nesebar, Tzarevo and Ahtopol after the incoming control.

3. The skipper on arrival in one of the above mentioned ports is obliged as soon as possible to visit the regional office of the Maritime Administration , supplied with a Temporary Navigation Certificate and certified Crew List from the Immigration Office and the Custom for the registration of the call.

4. Leaving the port is allowed by Maritime Administration only after specifying the next destination.

5. During the stay in Bulgarian internal and territorial waters is prohibited :

- the transportation and goods

- steering the yachts by persons in a drunken state

- doing diver operations without permission

- finishing subjects from the sea –bottom , which are cultural, historical or other valuables

- making any (no matter what) shots and explosives unless as distress signals

- all type of pollution of the sea environment .

6. It is prohibited to sail south from the parallel of Ahtopol's Lighthouse

7. Every change in the crew list to be done only after permission from the Emigration office in Varna .

8. Trespassers of these Regulations will be prosecuted according the laws of Republic of Bulgaria.

Figure 57

Bulgarian Regulations

available. A fisherman on the breakwater warned me of a sandbar in the entrance as I was going in. We took the dinghy to the pier and walked up to a gate where an old man finally said, "Hello and welcome", I think. I inquired about a restaurant and he pointed to a drive up the hill. The restaurant turned out to be very nice with a patio surrounded by a log wall. The entrance was flanked by a barnacle encrusted amphora and a large rusty anchor. I had fried shrimp and Bassem had a large fish. When he asked what kind of fish, the waitress gave a smile and pointed to the sea. So we knew that it came from the Black Sea. I topped off the dinner with a sinful chocolate fudge cake that was especially delicious. The bill came to 10 lev or about $6 USD.

The next day, on the way to Varna, I noticed that the U-bolt that attaches the roller furling headstay was broken. This happened once before, years ago, and I replaced it with a much larger bolt, which had now cracked. This bolt holds the forestay that supports the mast. Temporarily, I attached the main halyard to the bow to furnish a safety support for the mast. I planned to repair it permanently in the next port of Varna, Bulgaria, which was only 18 miles away. As luck would have it, we had a rare, beautiful south wind and I didn't dare use either sail without better mast support.

I could easily cope with these mechanical problems in addition to the wind and the waves but the human problems with the government authorities were intolerable. Their archaic, useless paperwork in high cost, government buildings frustrated me. Their multiple departments all wanted reams of forms filled in, stamped, and signed. This officialdom control was very trying. A captain on a homemade catamaran, Pilgrim's Progress, ahead of us lost his cool and really told them off.

Varna, Bulgaria to Constanta, Romania

On August 3rd we arrived in Varna, which is the second largest city in Bulgaria, the main naval base of the country, and a very large commercial port. We were welcomed by Port Police Officers and three Customs and Immigration Officers at the Varna Yacht Club. My paperwork was all in order and we didn't have any problems.

I replaced the broken U-bolt that held the forestay. There was a hole in the fore plate to use that was just the right size and angle. I had wanted to use it the last time I replaced the U-bolt but was voted down by the professional installer. I was attempting to do the whole job by myself when two Bulgarian bystanders came aboard and lent a hand, which made the job a lot easier and quicker. This was a very neighborly gesture on their part.

Thursday night Bassem was tired so I went out to dinner alone. The ABB Restaurant, with flashing red lights strung all around the trim, somehow caught my attention. I had scrod for dinner. This was a lot of very small fish, fried crispy and piled high on a platter. They had not been eviscerated and their eyes were glaring at me. They were delicious and I ate them like French fries. Figure 58 is a picture of a church that we visited in Varna.

Friday, August 6th, was a long day. I had to check out of Bulgaria and pay the Bulgarian exit fees, which took until 10:00 a.m., as we had to wait for the authorities. A large coal freighter (the Aristol) was waiting to unload and the Captain was furious at the delay. Then I had to sail 50 miles to Mangalia, Romania, and check in with the authorities there.

Figure 58
Church in Varna

Sailing up the north coast of Bulgaria, we passed a cape named Nos Kaliyakra that had very pretty red and white striped rocks. Figure 59 is a picture of this very significant cape. From this cape, all the way to Nos Sabla in Bulgaria, the rock cliffs tumble down into the sea to form a spectacular stretch of seacoast. We saw many tourists climbing, camping, swimming, and generally enjoying this beautiful coast. At Nos Sabla, there is an old, partially destroyed, oil dock that reaches far out to sea from the point. From there it is only a short distance to Romania where the land turns flat and featureless. Figure 60 is a picture of Bassem on the bow approaching Romania.

A Romanian Coast Guard boat met us at the border and called us on the VHF radio. They wanted to know the boat's name, last port, flag, and port of entrance to Romania. In the distance was the large city of Mangalia, Romania. When we entered, the port authorities were quick

Figure 59

Nos Kaliyakra Cape

and efficient, possibly because it was late Friday evening. We stopped at the Customs and Immigration Office on the commercial dock in the commercial harbor where I obtained the Romanian Permis de Plecare (Clearance Permit) shown in Figure 61. Figure 62 is a picture of me filling out the paperwork at the commercial dock and a picture of the Customs official, Angel who was very helpful. We were then directed to the inner yacht harbor. Against the advice of Bassem, I took a wrong turn and quickly grounded on a mud bottom. A couple on a large barge yelled and pointed the right way.

The yacht harbor contained one small fishing boat and no private sailboats or motorboats. This was unbelievable for a port at a large city on the sea. We later learned that, under the old communist regime, private citizens had not been allowed to own boats for fear that they might escape. As we approached the quay, a number of bystanders welcomed us and

At the commercial dock

Figure 60

Bassem on the bow

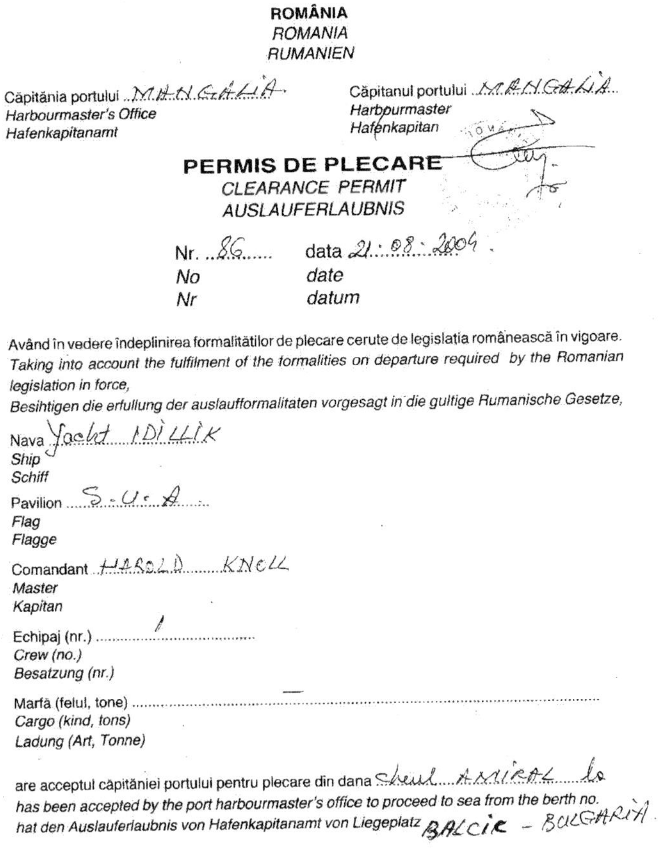

ROMÂNIA
ROMANIA
RUMANIEN

Căpitănia portului ..*M.A.N.G.A.L.I.A*.   Căpitanul portului ..*M.A.N.G.A.L.I.A*..
Harbourmaster's Office   *Harbourmaster*
Hafenkapitanamt   *Hafenkapitan*

PERMIS DE PLECARE
CLEARANCE PERMIT
AUSLAUFERLAUBNIS

Nr. ..*86*......   data *21 · 08 · 2004* ·
No   *date*
Nr   *datum*

Având în vedere îndeplinirea formalităților de plecare cerute de legislația românească în vigoare.
Taking into account the fulfilment of the formalities on departure required by the Romanian legislation in force,
Besihtigen die erfullung der auslaufformalitaten vorgesagt in die gultige Rumanische Gesetze,

Nava *Yacht IDILLIK*
Ship
Schiff

Pavilion ....*S·U·A*...
Flag
Flagge

Comandant ..*HAROLD KNELL*
Master
Kapitan

Echipaj (nr.) ..... */* ....
Crew (no.)
Besatzung (nr.)

Marfă (felul, tone) ....
Cargo (kind, tons)
Ladung (Art, Tonne)

are acceptul căpităniei portului pentru plecare din dana *Shtul AMIRAL la*
has been accepted by the port harbourmaster's office to proceed to sea from the berth no.
hat den Auslauferlaubnis von Hafenkapitanamt von Liegeplatz BALCIC - BULGARIA.

Figure 61

Romanian Clearance Permit

offered a hand to help us dock. After tying up to the dock we hunted up the Harbor Master who seemed glad to see us.

I found an ATM machine and purchased a few million Romanian lei (ROL). Then I bought some sausage, bread, and beer to take back to the boat. Romanian is a Romance language and many people even speak some French. I found that I could read the signs and communicate rather easily there, unlike Bulgaria, Turkey, and Greece. I tried to exchange my Bulgarian money for Romanian money at a dozen different places without

Figure 62
Customs paperwork

any luck. They would only take Euro and US dollars. We ate out and I had mussels, a salad, and an imported beer, Stella Artois, for 74,000 lei. This is about $2.25 USD.

The next day was overcast with a sprinkle of rain as we sailed to

Constanta, which is Romania's largest commercial port. We tied up to a pier at the Tomis Tourist Harbor where I had to sign the Immigration Rules for the harbor shown in Figures 63 and 64. Note that they do not allow women on board a boat and make the Captain responsible for crew's actions. There were only a few boats there and none of any consequence. There was a high beautiful fountain in the middle of the small harbor, which was very well protected behind large concrete breakwaters. Figure 65 is a picture of the harbor.

CONSTANTA IMMIGRATION OFFICE

RULES FOR TOMIS TOURIST HARBOR

1. The employees of Constanta Immigration Office wear badges with titles and names and they represent the authority in matters concerning: passports, foreign citizens, boarding, visas, and they are authorized to perform controls and examinations at any time during the day or at night in order to ensure compliance with these rules.
2. As far as the arrival formalities are concerned, the master of the vessel (yacht) must declare all the people on board, crewmembers, passengers, stowaways, etc.
3. The access on board of all vessels stationed in Tomis Harbor is allowed only based on official documents issued and approved by the Immigration Office.
   The access on board of these vessels is denied to women and to any individual known for his involvement in activities that might affect the order and security on board of the vessels.
4. Once the arrival/departure control is completed, if any other person that was not declared at the time the vessel entered the port is found on board, the ship's master must retain that person and inform the Immigration Office immediately by calling 0241/616320 or 0241/601233.
5. The access of sailors and passengers ashore is allowed only under the circumstances provided by law. If any of the members of the crew or the master knows about a sailor who left the city, they must inform the Immigration Office immediately by calling the numbers mentioned above.
6. Any passenger or crewmember that leaves the vessel shall carry his passport or seaman's book, together with the shore passes issued by the Immigration Office upon the vessel's arrival in Tomis Harbor.
7. The ship's master (or yacht's master) must inform the Immigration Office when a passenger or crewmember goes in the city and does not return on board of the vessel. When the passenger or the sailor does not return until the vessel's departure, the master shall submit a letter

Figure 63
Tomis Harbor Rules

71

of guarantee where he accepts the responsibility of covering the costs that might occur as a result of the illegal stay of the foreign citizen in Romania.

8. It is the ship's master's responsibility to have the whole crew and all the passengers on board when the Immigration Office requires the departure of the vessel either by phone or by using the Border Police agent on duty in Tomis Harbor.

9. Any operation of signing on, signing off or transfer of the sailors shall be performed in due time, at the request of the ship's master, by informing the Customs authorities and the Harbor Master's Office and only after the approval of the Immigration Office was granted.

10. Non-observance, violation or elusion of the rules mentioned above, regardless of the circumstances, shall be punished with criminal or administrative sanctions, as the case may be.

11. No person shall be allowed on board of the vessel, regardless of its status, without the approval of the Chief of the Border Crossing Point, unless this person is part of the ship's crew or the passengers list.

Date: 07.08.2004   Ship's Master,

Harold Knoll

Figure 64
Tomis Harbor Rules

Figure 65
Constanta Marina

Figure 66
Jurgen and Liller Meyer Helm

I spent part of the evening with a Danish-German couple, Jurgen and Liller Meyer Helm. They needed help in finding an Internet café so I walked with them to find one. Afterwards, we had a good meal at a Turkish restaurant. They are a very interesting couple from Sanso, Denmark. They sold their home to pay for their trip through the Kiel Kanal, the Elba River, the Rhone River, and the Danube River to the Black Sea on their nicely furnished motorboat. Figure 66 is a picture of them with their boat.

The next day I arose to a clear sky and a bright sun. After Bassem left early for Bucharest, I explored Constanta and found the statue of Ovid, who was exiled here from Rome in 8 AD. I visited the Muzel National de Istorie Si Archoalogie (Natural History and Archaeological Museum). It contained statues and artifacts from the Neolithic up to the Roman and Greek periods. I'm always impressed by the amount of gold that the ancient people had. Many of the statues had been buried to preserve them from being destroyed by the Christians. The museum was a classic with antique rugs covering the floors, dusty displays, and hot muggy temperatures. I was afraid that I would become mummified by the heat and oppressive air. I also visited the Banca National a Romaniei, where it took five persons to cash my Euro Check. There were two who gave directions, one who did the bookwork, a cashier to give me the small change and another cashier at another window for the large bills. The exchange rate was 34,500,000 lei to $1 USD. In 1997, the rate was 7,048 to the USD. Inflation hit really hard in Romania.

On Tuesday I asked some workers who were raking the grass along the waterfront for directions to the Aquarium. They pointed to an impressive looking building in the far distance down the shore. I walked along the beautiful waterfront overlooking the breaking waves of the Black Sea all the way to this building. The building was a casino that was very old and ornate but in wonderful condition. Across the sidewalk and street was a low, unimpressive and rundown building with the Aquarium sign on it. I entered the door and was met by a sign and a lady asking for a 30,000 lei entry fee. I paid and was given a little booklet of pictures. The aquarium tanks were scummy but contained some interesting fish. Most of the fish were identified as being from America. There was only one large tank that held native fish, such as sturgeon and flatfish, from the Black Sea.

On Wednesday, August 11th, I thought that the country was being invaded! The army, navy, and marines started arriving by ship. There were over thirty naval ships of all kinds. Air Force planes were constantly flying just above the water and then buzzing the city. Small rubber boats were launched with fully armed Navy Seals. All this was happening on the seaward side of the pier that "Idyllic" was tied up to! Figures

67 and 68 are pictures of the marines marching at the marina. Next, a large planeload of paratroopers was dropped just offshore amongst some rubber boats and a helicopter landed on the pier. That day Constanta was celebrating a combination of Marinea Day and Santa Maria Day. All of the parks and the dock had been spruced up and flowers had been planted. Even the bollards in the marina had been painted luminescent red as shown in Figure 69.

For dinner that night, I had a steak with all of the trimmings and an expensive Danish beer. This cost me 120,000 lei or about $3 USD. This is the least expensive place in the world that I have found. The next day I walked about five kilometers to an Internet café and then to the Stampile Express store. At each port, the officials had always asked me to officially stamp their forms, so I bought a stamp with my name and the name of the boat, "Idyllic", on it.

Figure 67
Marines marching at the marina

Figure 68
Marines marching at the marina

Figure 69
Painting the bollards

I had originally planned to meet my next crewmember, Harold Byler, in Odessa, Ukraine. He had obtained a visa to the Ukraine before he left the USA. Upon arrival in Constanta, I had learned that since my crewmember, Bassem, had a Jordanian passport, he would not be able to get a Ukrainian visa. Furthermore, I had learned that I might not be allowed in myself without a letter of invitation from a Ukrainian citizen. I had e-mailed Byler and we had agreed to meet in Chisinau, Moldova instead of Odessa. We had checked and there was good train service from both Odessa and Constanta, and Moldovan visas were available to US citizens free. Chisinau sounded like an interesting place; it is the capital of the poorest country in the world at this time.

After finding out that there isn't a Moldovan Consul in Constanta, I took a train to Bucharest, the capital of Romania, to get a visa to Moldova. I spent the night at the Elvis Villa Hostal for 369,000 lei. Finding my way around in Bucharest was very difficult. Most of the information that I obtained was incorrect. The city is very old and not even the taxi drivers seem to know the streets. The city is very large and spread out. Figure 70 is a picture of a Bucharest street scene. There doesn't seem to be any shortage of space. Buildings are scattered here and there with large areas of green space and parks. The tourist attractions are miles apart and walking from one to another is almost impossible. The University Hospital occupies a square mile, as does the Palace of Parliament, the second largest office building in the world, shown in Figures 71 and 72.

Before WWII, Bucharest was known as the Paris of the Balkans but its glory now lies under the grime and decay of neglect and political turmoil. Communist dictator from (1965-1989), Nicolae Ceausescu, initiated maniacal development of the capital that forced the displacement of many thousands of citizens and bankrupted the country. He left many half-

Figure 70
Bucharest street scene

Figure 71
Palace of Parliment

Figure 72
University Hospital

built buildings and cranes standing idle in fenced-in areas surrounded by a boulevard lined with trees. This diverted resources away from streets, sidewalks, sewers, and water projects desperately needed, especially out in the country. There are villages in the country with very small houses with enclosed yards where vegetables are grown and chickens and goats are raised. Cows are staked out individually. Most of the transportation there is by horse cart down the dirt tracks through the center of the village.

The Danow (Danube) River, which crosses the country between Bucharest and Constanta, has been channeled for commerce. One nuclear plant was observed with only one unit out of four working; the others were idle for repair. They had been idle for years and probably will be for years to come.

I was unable to find the Moldovan Embassy in Bucharest. I walked for hours trying to find it and became exhausted. I missed Bassem at our agreed meeting place, the Peoples' Palace (Palace of Parliament). I finally got a taxi to the Gare Nord (North Train Station). In only a short distance, the taxi had run up a bill of 300,000 lei, which was all the money that I had left for the entire day's trip. A previous long taxi ride had only cost 89,000 lei. I yelled for him to stop and began to protest. I wound up without any money left and walking nowhere near the Gare Nord.

I walked to the Metro station and, with the small change that I found in the bottom of my backpack, boarded the underground railroad to the Gare Nord for 20,000 lei. Arriving, I was told to go to the casa for a billet (ticket). After a long wait in line, I was told that I need another 20,000 lei for a seat even though I already had a return ticket to Constanta. I offered to sell my watch but a bystander gave me his last 20,000 lei to buy my seat. So much for all the talk about the bad people of Romania.

The trip back was interesting. I shared a compartment with five other passengers. Two of them were seamen with their wives who didn't speak any English. One passenger, Dan, was a ship's electrician and had just returned from Singapore. He sails on freighters, repairing their electrical systems while they are at sea. Figure 73 is a picture of Romanian visitors to "Idyllic".

Constanta attracts both Romanian and international tourists. There seemed to be a constant parade of people passing the "Idyllic" and stopping for pictures and a try at the English language. I felt sometimes as if I was on display. An occasional tourist jumps on board just to be able to say that they were on an American boat. While relaxing, I occasionally invited a few on board and showed them around just for fun as most had never been on a sailboat and were surprised at what they saw. The harbor had a very small ferryboat that gave rides. They were always overloaded and had a big siren blasting away to attract more riders.

Monday, I helped the Dutch couple on their boat, the "Alegria",

Beach at Constanta

Figure 73
Romanian visitors

Figure 74
The "Academic Star"

leave the dock bound for Balchik, Bulgaria, in a windstorm with high seas. The Dutch are good sailors and they shouldn't have had any problems. The temperature today is 68 degrees; the first time below 70 for me this summer. I visited the "Academic Star", which is a training vessel for future captains. The captain, Nick, showed me around the old, decrepit sailboat that has a rough fiberglass covering. Figure 74 is a picture of this boat. He is very proud of his boat and his program. I first met him when his engine failed and a navy tugboat pulled him in. I helped him get to shore. He asked me all of the usual questions and we had a cup of vodka before he left to participate in the Marine Day festival.

In spite of all the people jumping on and off my boat, I didn't have anything taken. A German boat nearby had many children diving off and climbing around on the boat. This caused some minor damage that was done without any ill intent. The only time I yelled at anyone was when I was sleeping and they woke me up bouncing the rubber fenders on the side of the boat. Many of the ladies seemed to enjoy getting down on their knees and peeking through the windows at me. I installed a new fuel gauge but it still doesn't work. Maybe it's the sending unit in the tank again. It stopped working once before about three years ago. Things seem to break faster than I can fix them.

Harold Byler should have arrived on the train but he didn't show up and I was unable to contact him by e-mail. I really wondered where he was since I was supposed to meet him in Chisinau, Moldova.

Finally, after midnight on Wednesday night, he showed up and rapped on the side of the boat to wake me up. I was very glad to see him, as I was afraid that something bad had happened to him. He was exhausted and we immediately went to sleep for the night. Figure 75 shows my route from Istanbul, Turkey to Constanta, Romania.

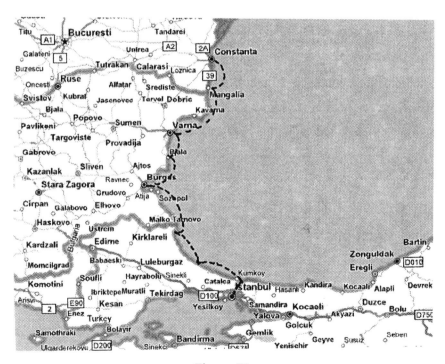

Figure 75
Route from Istanbul to Constanta

Odessa, Ukraine to Constanta, Romania

> The apparent length of a boat is inversely
> proportional to the height of the waves.
>
> Harold Byler

Although I had a 14-day transit visa to the Ukraine, my crewmember, Bassem, had a Jordanian passport and could not obtain a Ukrainian visa. There were local people in Constanta who wanted to crew for me but, having Romanian passports, were also not allowed in the Ukraine. This meant that, in order to meet Harold Byler in Odessa as originally planned, I would have to sail over two days and nights into a strange port by myself. I considered this to be a bit risky. Byler and I then hastily planned to meet, by train, in Chisinau, Moldova, which promised to be an interesting trip.

On August 13th, Byler drove from his home in Brady, Texas, to Brownwood, Texas, where he flew on Mesa Airlines to Dallas, Texas. He spent the night in Dallas and then flew on Northwest Airlines from Dallas to Detroit, Michigan, to Amsterdam, Netherlands, to Istanbul, Turkey. From Istanbul he flew to Odessa, Ukraine on Turkish Airlines. He had obtained a one year Ukrainian visa before leaving the US. This trip was without incident and he arrived just at dusk. He took a taxi to a hotel that he had found listed on the Internet.

August is the vacation month in Europe and Byler discovered that the hotel was full. When he returned to the taxi, it was gone since the entry to each of these hotels is a long walk from the street through a walled garden. In the dark now and without transportation, Byler had to resort to a local custom that he had read about, of standing on the curb with a hand held out, palm down. Most of the drivers will then stop and give you a ride if they're going your way. A price, usually about half that of a taxi, has to be negotiated before entering the vehicle. Byler had been warned about entering a vehicle with more than one person in it and exiting quickly if another person entered. A large number of people in Odessa use this system of traveling. The drivers need the money and are eager to give rides.

Byler discovered that the language barrier in the Ukraine is complete. During his stay there, he was unable to find anybody who spoke English or any sign not in Cyrillic. This made communication almost impossible. He managed to locate a couple of other hotels which were also full, but traveling alone in the dark in Odessa is considered dangerous and he was beginning to get desperate to find a place to sleep since midnight was approaching and he was carrying his luggage. At the "Magnolia Hotel" he was turned down again but the guard at the front door was sympathetic and convinced the woman at the front desk to give him a room.

The resort hotels along the beach area in Odessa are mostly old sanitoriums with spa facilities. These hotels are very old and rapidly decaying from their original opulent condition. This seemed to be true of almost all of the Ukraine. It still has its old, Russian, communist heritage. As a result, the country is poor and not progressive. The rooms at the Magnolia were all suites consisting of a hall door entering into a small alcove connecting two very small (about 7x10-foot) bedrooms. This alcove also connects to separate bath and toilet rooms. Byler had to share his "suite" with a vacationing couple and their two small children squeezed into the other bedroom.

Byler's room was on the 10th floor of the 12-story building. Each bedroom had an overhanging balcony facing the sea with a lovely view; however, he was afraid to go out on the balcony as it had large cracks in the concrete floor. The door to the balcony would not close completely and the room must be windy and cold during their bitter winters. However, during his stay it was quite warm without air-conditioning in the 85-degree temperatures. The mattress had broken springs sticking up that were covered by a tablecloth under the sheet. Toilet paper and soap were not supplied and he had to locate a small store the next day to purchase some.

The room cost him 40 USD per day, which included three meals in the hotel restaurant. He said that the restaurant was the one thing that he enjoyed in the Ukraine. It was very nicely decorated and had excellent food. It seated about one hundred people and most of the hotel's occupants ate there. He was assigned a seat the first morning and was thereafter led to the same seat for each meal. Breakfast was served starting at 9:00 a.m., lunch at 2:00 p.m., and dinner at 9:00 p.m. Each meal started with a large bowl of borsch (cabbage soup). Byler was pleased to discover that the soup, being well seasoned and containing other things besides cabbage, was very good.

At breakfast the borsch was followed by a plate of lettuce, sliced tomatoes and cucumbers accompanied by a plate of sliced lunchmeat and cheeses. Then came a bowl of cubed fresh fruit and melon. There was fresh bread and butter on the table along with a small bowl of salt, a small bowl of curry powder, and a container of sugar. Diners dipped out the salt with the handle of their fork and sprinkled it on their food. Next, there was bacon, eggs, and fried potatoes with toast and honey. Cereal was available and there was a bowl of tea bags along with a large thermos of hot water. Service was very good. The other meals were equally complete and delicious.

The day after arriving was Sunday and Byler rested from his trip and the eight-hour jet lag. In the afternoon, he started exploring the city. The south shore of the city where the resort hotels were located had a long sandy beach at the bottom of the bluffs. The hotels were up on the bluffs with many long sets of steps going down. The walk down from the hotels to the beach and back up was very tiring. Figure 76 shows part of this walk to the beach. Figure 77 is a picture of the beach where there were a few fast food and drinks places.

The streets in Odessa ran at odd angles and getting lost on any trip was almost a certainty. Figure 87 shows one of the better residential streets. Traffic on the rough cobblestone streets was heavy and the cars drove up to 70 mph weaving in and out to dodge pedestrians. The people in Ukraine drove faster that anywhere Byler had ever been and the old cars took a terrible bashing and beating. The ancient trolley cars, such as the one shown in Figure 79, were free, but jam-packed with additional passengers pushing and shoving to get on. There was a dilapidated bus system for a nominal charge but the destinations (in Cyrillic) of these buses were undecipherable. About half of the people, including young girls and well-dressed older people, used the hand-out, palm-down, hitchhiking system. An attempt to locate an Internet café was unsuccessful; however, he did find a local grocery store. Food seemed to be very important and this store was no exception. Figure 80 shows the fresh and smoked seafood counter. Figure 81 shows the cheese counter and Figure 82 shows the meat and sausage counter. Byler said that he would kill for a store like that in his small hometown in West Texas.

Byler said that when approached, people seemed genuinely friendly and tried to be helpful but the language barrier was just too much. The people appeared to be mostly poor and their standard of living was not too good. Some people, in the distant past before the revolution, must

Figure 76
Walk to the beach

Figure 77
Beach at Odessa

Figure 78
Residential street

Figure 79
Odessa trolley car

Figure 80
Seafood counter

Figure 81
Cheese counter

Figure 82
Meat counter

Figure 83
Homes in Odessa

have been very wealthy judging by their mansions that are now decaying. Figure 83 shows two of these homes.

Early the next day, Monday August 16th, Byler checked out of the Magnolia Hotel and managed to find the railroad station. This was a very large and stately building in front of a large traffic circle with a tall monument. After standing in line for an hour with his luggage, he attempted to purchase a ticket to Chisinau, Moldova, where we were to meet. The clerk looked at his passport, checked a list, and asked for his Moldavian visa that he didn't have yet. He was informed that he had to have the visa to purchase a ticket. He then spent the morning in various lines trying to obtain a visa only to discover that Moldova, being the poorest country in Europe, did not have consulates but only embassies in major capitals. The nearest embassy was in the capital city of, Kiev, Ukraine, which is a day's train ride each way from Odessa plus a day to find the embassy and get a visa. Meanwhile, I was finding out the same thing back in Constanta, Romania. We were not going to be able to meet in Chisinau as planned and we didn't have any way to communicate!

The only direct highway from Odessa to Constanta goes across about five miles of Moldova and was therefore unavailable to Byler without a Moldovian visa. Ukrainians were not required to have a Moldavian visa. There aren't any trains going up the east side of Moldova and a bus ride would have been impossible because of the many connections between the small towns. There weren't any direct highways on that route. Byler took a taxi to the airport and found that there was only one airline connection on a small airline to Bucharest, Romania, for a high price, which was booked solid five days in advance. The situation appeared hopeless!

On the drive back into the city, the taxi driver began to understand the problem and suddenly swung off the main street into some narrow side streets, finally stopping on a back street in front of a small house with a gate in the makeshift sheet-tin wall. It gave Byler quite a scare when another man without a shirt came out to join them. The other man turned out to be the driver's 23-year-old son. He went into the house and returned with a road map that they consulted and discussed in Russian at great length. Finally they made Byler understand that they were proposing to drive him in the taxi up the east side of Moldova to northern Ukraine and then across the top of Moldova to a town on the west side of Ukraine that had a train station. This would be a taxi trip of about 600 miles and then a 500-mile trip on the train down eastern Romania to Bucharest followed by a 120-mile bus trip to Constanta. The taxi driver was worried that Byler would not be allowed into Romania without a visa. The Ukrainians cannot obtain a Romanian visa (and vice versa) due to an ongoing dispute between the two. Byler had determined via the Internet before leaving the U.S. that, being a U.S. citizen, he did not need a visa to visit Romania. Not being sure where they might really take him, Byler declined the taxi trip.

After one more unproductive trip back to the train station, where the taxi driver assisted him, Byler re-evaluated his situation and, in desperation, decided to go. One factor was that this taxi was a nearly new, full-sized Mitsubishi. Figure 84 is a picture of this taxi. Byler negotiated the asking price of $350 USD down to $250 USD and they returned to the taxi driver's house so the driver could take a shower, change clothes, and pick up his son who would share the driving. The taxi driver's wife prepared them a very nice lunch preceded by the usual large bowl of delicious borsch. While the lunch was being prepared, the son, Sereja, showed Byler his computer and gave him his sister, Violetta's, Internet address since he didn't have an Internet server himself.

Figure 84
Mitsubishi taxi

Then they were off, literally! The son drove. His dad was teaching him to drive. He proudly explained that he had been driving for three years. He drove 170 –190 kph (translates to 100-120 mph). There wasn't any seatbelt in the back seat and Byler was terrified but afraid to say anything because they might get mad and drop him off in the middle of nowhere. The roads were bad, lumpy asphalt with lots of construction and potholes. The truck and car traffic was heavy and Sereja weaved in and out, passing in front of trucks and often forcing them to hit the brakes. He would pass a line of cars in front of an oncoming truck and then squeeze into line at the last moment. He was just skipping along on the high spots of the road and bottoming out on all of the potholes, bouncing from side to side. He straightened out the right angle, dirt construction, detour jogs without slowing down. This continued for eleven hours. Byler was a nervous wreck when they finally arrived at a train station in Cernivici, Ukraine.

They stopped only once, for lunch, where Sereja bought some sunflower seeds that he proceeded to pick out and eat with one hand while he drove with the other hand. Small villages had a 40km speed posted on a tree entering the village. There would usually be a policeman in the village who would step out and wave a black and white wand at speeders who are required to stop immediately. The driving son would jam on the brakes upon seeing one of the signs. Then, if no policeman was evident, he would step on the gas again. He got stopped several times. He would get out, walk with the policeman back behind the car, and give him a one-dollar USD bribe. The policeman would then wave us on. The young man would then stand on the gas pedal in low gear and throw rocks everywhere as he spun the wheels leaving.

The land in the country was basically all flat, cleared farmland. There weren't any fences and the fields were very large. The fields ranged from 100-500 acres each, which a few years ago had been collective farms. They are still operated as cooperative farms with the profit, if any, going to the farmers now instead of to the government. There is some question as to exactly who owns what land. What little farm equipment he saw was very old and most of the farming was being done by hand. There were a lot of horse drawn wagons in use. The villages and the farmhouses were small and very poor.

At dark, the father started driving and he drove just like his son, only in the dark. On the north side of Moldova, he started stopping in the larger towns and enquiring about trains. Finally, upon reaching the city of Cernivici, Ukraine, about midnight, he found a train station with a posted train to Bucharest. This was all in Cyrillic, but the driver assured Byler, by waving his arms and pointing, that a ticket on the 6:00 a.m. train to Bucharest could be purchased at Window No. 3 when it opened at 5:00

a.m.. Byler paid the driver and they left to drive straight back to Odessa.

Byler spent the night on one of the crowded benches in the railroad station and was at Window No. 3 promptly at 5:00 a.m. The clerk looked at his U.S. passport, consulted a list, and issued him a ticket costing 40 USD for the 6:00 a.m. train on track 6 to Bucharest. On the ancient train, he discovered that he would have to share a small 6-foot by 6-foot sleeping compartment with a Bulgarian woman and her teenage daughter. Unfortunately, the daughter had a very bad cold. The window in the compartment was not designed to be opened and he was sure that he would get her cold (but somehow he didn't). The woman had a large, cold bottle of beer that she insisted on sharing. Byler had half a bottle of Ukrainian red wine in his backpack that he, in turn, shared. The woman was very talkative but didn't speak a word of English. Figure 85 is a picture of the Bulgarian woman and her daughter in the sleeping compartment.

After about an hour, they reached the Romanian border where the train was parked on a siding while the border guards searched the train from top to bottom, searched all of the luggage, and examined everyone's papers a number of times. The passengers had to fill out a form declaring, among other things, the amount of money they were bringing into Romania. Without actually counting the money in his concealed money belt, Byler took a guess and listed it. Later, a customs woman came in and asked to see the money. She then counted it carefully and found a very small discrepancy. When he offered to change the list to correct it, she got very upset and called the other officials. Finally they left and nothing happened regarding this incident. After four hours of bureaucracy, the train was eventually cleared and crossed the border bound for Bucharest. The Bulgarian woman had come prepared for the trip and had brought a very generous lunch that she also insisted on sharing. After they ate

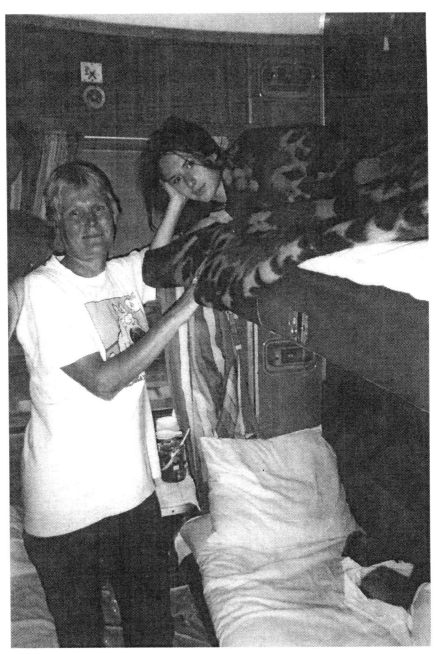

Figure 85
Bulgarian woman and daughter

the lunch, she and her daughter went to the rest room where they changed into their pajamas and then came back and went to bed. So Byler lay down on the bunk and got three hours of badly needed sleep.

Byler said that the countryside on the eastern side of Romania was flat farmland very similar to that of the Ukraine. Figures 86 and 87 show some of these fields. They didn't seem to have any type of hay baler but stacked their hay around a vertical pole. Some fields were covered with these small haystacks. The farming was done mostly by hand with the help of horses. There were a few sheep and goats but almost no cattle. Figure 88 is a picture of the only cattle that he saw. Figure 89 is a picture of typical farmhouses; Figure 90 shows country villages; and Figure 91 shows transportation in the country.

They arrived in Bucharest just before dark and Byler, with the help of some Romanians who spoke English, was able to find a minibus to Constanta for 12 USD. Figure 92 shows a street in Bucharest. Arriving in Constanta, after stopping to eat a light supper along the way, he enlisted a taxi driver to help him locate the "Idyllic". Constanta has a large commercial port but practically no yacht facilities and it was after midnight before they found the "Idyllic" and me. Figure 93 shows Byler's route from Odessa, Ukraine to Constanta, Romania.

Figure 94 shows the "Idyllic" in the harbor at Constanta, Romania. There are few yachting facilities in the Black Sea because, under the communist rule, citizens were not permitted to own boats and the Sea was closed to foreign pleasure boats. Only commercial fishermen could get the special permits required. The few privately owned boats that we saw there were mostly very crudely made but nevertheless the owners were very proud of them.

Figure 86
Sunflower fields in Romania

Figure 87
Hay fields in Romania

Figure 88
Cattle on farm in Romania

Figure 89
Farmhouses in Romania

Figure 90
Country villages in Romania

Figure 91
Transportation in the farm country

Figure 92
Street in Bucharest

Figure 93
Byler's route from Odessa to Constanta

Figure 94
"Idyllic" in Constanta harbor

Constanta, Romania to Burgas, Bulgaria

When we woke up Wednesday morning, August 18th, we immediately went to an Internet café to let everybody know that Harold Byler was OK. I had gotten everybody upset by inquiring about his whereabouts when he didn't show up on time. I guided him back through town, showing him an interesting mosque and the History Museum. We had breakfast at McDonald's. Their breakfast was different from their U.S. menu, so I had a Big Mac and Harold had a Pork Mac.

We returned to the boat where I picked up some money. Then we returned to town to buy groceries. Harold went wild when he saw the prices of the wine and bought an entire case that he lugged a few kilometers back to the boat. We then took a short snooze to recover.

On the way to dinner that night, I took Harold around the waterfront to see the sights. Just after passing the casino, shown in Figure 95, two young gypsy men approached us on the street and started asking questions in fairly good English. Two other gypsy men soon joined them and before we knew what was happening, they went for our billfolds. Harold yelled to me and we started kicking, swinging, running, and yelling. There were some other people on the street, so the Gypsies gave up and left.

We stopped at a Turkish restaurant and had a delicious beef kabob. The food in this part of the world is wonderful. Finding our way back to the boat was a problem as the streets are unlit and full of broken pavement and potholes. Harold slipped and fell in one place but wasn't hurt.

The next day we left Constanta after checking out with the Harbor Master, Customs and Immigration, Harbor Security, and Port Police.

Figure 95
Waterfront Casino in Constanta, Romania

They had to be sure that we didn't have any stowaways on board. Figure 96 is a picture of the Port Policeman with his son, checking us out. Harold Byler is sitting in the background. After leaving the harbor, we passed the longest breakwater and commercial dock that we had ever seen. It was about 12 miles long. A small part of it is shown in Figure 97. We picked up a fairly good northwest wind and sailed most of the day until the wind died about 4:00 p.m.

We entered the port of Mangalia, Romania, and tied up at Customs on a commercial dock where we went through the reverse process that we had completed leaving Constanta. The port policeman asked for a ride over to the town quay, which we gladly offered. He was a very pleasant fellow and talked all of the way across the harbor. He seemed to be excited about his first ride in a sailboat.

Arriving alongside the town quay, we tied up and immediately hooked up to the electric box on the dock. There wasn't any electricity and we discovered that the wiring to the box ended about 100 feet up the dock. Shortly, some workmen came and removed the box and the wiring. They were in the process of replacing all of the boxes and installing new wiring. They completed this a few minutes before we left the dock two days later.

Looking over the side of the boat, we noticed six inches of beautiful green seaweed growing along the waterline on the side of the boat, which explained why the boat had been sailing a little slower than usual. We took the boat back over to the commercial dock where we had more room to work and there was a little current to carry away the debris. I put on a mask and flippers and went over the side. Harold rigged a line alongside and held it for me as I worked down the side cleaning seaweed off the hull. Fortunately it didn't go far below the waterline.

Figure 96
Port Policeman and son

Figure 97
Commercial pier in Constanta, Romania

Going to the other side, we made an interesting discovery: the seaweed was only on one side of the boat! The other side was covered with barnacles instead! This must have been due to being tied up in the same position, relative to the sun, for a relatively long period of time while waiting for Harold in Constanta. Later, comparing notes with Captain Jon, he said that he had had the same problem and had to work for a whole day cleaning his hull. The Black Sea seems conducive to this growth of marine life on boat hulls. I worked for several hours trying to remove the barnacles without much success. This attracted a large school of fish that became more numerous and bold as I worked. I was exhausted by the time I finished.

Later that evening, I e-mailed my friend Dan, the ship's electrician from Mangalia, who had loaned me some money back in Constanta. He showed up at the boat and asked if I had any electrical problems. Three years ago, I had installed a 220-volt system and my 110-volt system hadn't worked since. I explained this to him and he offered to fix it. He left to get some wire and equipment. His name is Dan Preda Nicolae. The next day he showed up with an assortment of wire and equipment. He worked an hour or more stringing wire and finally announced the problem solved. He then let me know that he was interested in finding a job in the USA. I promised to help him. Byler, having experience with resumes, put together a form for him to fill out. Dan was another example of the friendly and helpful Romanians.

Mangalia was a very pleasant place with many nice facilities: a convenient dock, a good Internet café, a very complete grocery store, several very good restaurants, and a beautiful topless beach, which is shown in Figure 98. We hated to leave, but needed to get on down the coast before the fall storms began. Leaving for Balcik, Bulgaria, we proceeded down the coast and, for the first time in my life, I actually went

Figure 98
Beach in Mangalia, Romania

into the wrong port! I knew upon entering that it was wrong, as it did not fit the description in the Crusing Guide. Also, there weren't any customs officials waiting on the dock. It was Golden Sands, the resort port next to Varna. I had taken my GPS position from the wrong page. One mistake in a lifetime ain't bad!

Approaching the town quay, we were waved over to the fishing dock. We had some difficulty tying up at the dock, as some fishermen next to us didn't seem to want us to tie up alongside them. They wanted us to drop an anchor and back in to the dock. Due to the language barrier, we didn't understand that they were about to leave and we were in their way. The harbormaster asked for 10 lei. I only had a 20 lei note. He promised to return with the change but never did.

We took a cool walk to the town, which was full of tourists from the boats tied up to the quay. We ate an excellent fish dinner and walked up the street to a deli. Lightening was flashing all around and big raindrops were starting to fall, so we hurried back to the boat. The storm intensified to terrific proportions and I was glad that we were securely tied up in port. The broadside wind heeled the "Idyllic" over stretching the dock lines steel taut. I yelled to a couple that had taken refuge behind the hull of a nearby boat but, in the howling wind, they apparently didn't understand my invitation of shelter.

We left the next day after paging the security guard. Unbelievably, there weren't any customs, port police or permission required to leave. We used the iron sails on flat seas in intense heat along the most beautiful coast of the entire trip. High massive rock cliffs disappeared down into the blue sea hundreds of feet below. The rocks were multicolored: red, yellow, brown, and white. They contrasted with the green vegetation on top of the cliffs. There were many tourists on the rocks and climbers rappelling down the cliffs. Others were swimming and sunbathing at small, secluded beaches. This was one of nature's playgrounds. Part of this coast is shown in Figure 99.

We went into the small yacht harbor at Varna and tied up alongside the pier just in front of Jon's boat, "S.Y. Kahuringl". Figure 100 is a picture of Jon's boat in Varna. Figure 101 is a picture of "Idyllic" in Varna. I gave Harold a short tour of the city including the old church there shown in Figure 102. There is a pedestrian tunnel used to cross under the busy street. Figure 103 shows a street in Varna and Figure 104 is a picture of me at the very interesting Naval Museum in Varna.

While we were there, Harold did his laundry in the lavatory in the men's rest room at the harbor office shown behind the "Idyllic" in Figure 101. He hung the laundry out to dry on the "Idyllic"'s lifelines. Laundry is always a problem as we are usually only in port for one day and with a foreign language barrier, it's hard to find a laundry with same day service.

Figure 99
Bulgarian seacoast

Figure 100
Jon's boat "S.Y.Kahuringl" in Varna

Figure 101
"Idyllic" in Varna

Figure 102
Old church in Varna, Bulgaria

Figure 103
Street in Varna, Bulgaria

Figure 104
Knoll at the Naval Museum in Varna

Figure 105
Approaching Point Emona

Figure 106
Knoll rounding Point Emona

Figure 107
Harbor in Nesebar

About two or three miles offshore, approaching the Nos Emine Cape between Byala and Nesebar, a small brown bird flew into the cabin. He flew in and out several times and then lit in the Vee birth where he rested for a couple of hours. When we got closer to shore and he could see the green hills and trees, he flew away towards land. Figure 105 is a picture taken approaching Point Emona. Figure 106 is a picture of me rounding Point Emona.

We entered the yacht harbor at Nesebar and tied up to a small dock. Figure 107 shows the harbor at Nesebar. We walked across the causeway to the old town out on the peninsula that was built on Greek and Roman ruins. Nesebar is a popular spot for Bulgarian tourists. UNESCO declared it to be an architectural and archaeological reserve. There are many ancient churches, walls, and buildings constructed with multicolored stones and bricks. Figure 108 is a picture of one of the churches and Figure 109 is one of the buildings. We ate on the patio of a restaurant in a restored ancient building overlooking the fisherman's harbor. Music was provided by an accordian-guitar duo. Figure 110 is a picture of the restaurant. We had smoked fish salad, beefsteak with onions, and Stella Atois beer for 38 lev or about $25 USD combined. This was the highest price that we paid all summer. We visited some of the tourist shops where Harold looked for a gift for his wife. Figure 111 shows street dancers in Nesebar and Figure 112 shows a bagpipe player there.

The next morning we sailed to Burgas, a large city and a major commercial port. We tied up to the commercial pier at Burgas right under the stern of a large freighter unloading wheat. We were met by a hot, tired official who gave a quick look at our papers, asked a few of the usual questions, and left with our papers for his air-conditioned office. We sat in the shade and waited for over an hour before he came back and sent

Figure108
Ancient church in Nesebar

Figure 109
Ancient building in Nesebar

Figure 110
Restaurant in Nesebar

Figure 111
Street dancers

Figure 112
Bagpipe player

Figure 113
Walking the gangplank

us across the bay to the tugboat dock to check in with the Harbor Master there. Figure 113 shows me walking the gangplank at the dock.

We went into town where, as in some other major cities in Bulgaria, the main streets downtown had been closed to vehicles. This allowed a lot of room for pedestrians and these streets were full of shoppers. I think a lot of U.S. cities could use this concept to revitalize their downtown shopping. We enjoyed watching the people and looking in the shops. At the major street intersections where there was a plaza, traditional bands and dancers in costumes were providing entertainment for the public, which is another great idea. Some of the dancers are shown in Figure 114.

I saw three boys grab a woman's shopping bags and run off. She screamed and chased them. I also chased them but was unable to catch up with them and they lost me in the side streets. I understand that this is a somewhat common occurrence in both Bulgaria and Romania. The police were called but arrived too late to be effective.

Jon showed up in his boat and tied up to the tugboat quay right behind us. Together, we occupied about 120 feet of the quay. The pilot boats and tugboats were having to raft up at the quay due to lack of space. We knew that we would probably have to leave to make room and sure enough, the dock master asked Jon to move to the yacht harbor, which is about a two-kilometer walk from town and very inconvenient. Jon had to move his boat right away but we happened to be away when the dock master came. We came back late and promised to leave promptly at 7:00 a.m., which we did. That morning we were fogged in and barely managed to find our way to the end of the harbor where the Yacht Club was. Figure 115 shows the boats tied up at the Yacht Club in Burgas. Jon's boat is in the background and the "Idyllic" is on the left. Figure 116 is a stern view of Jon's boat. Figure 117 shows a street in Burgas and Figure 118 is a view of a side street there.

We soon discovered that the 110/220-volt electrical problem had not been solved after all and the 110-volt system still didn't work. After we cooked a breakfast of bacon and toast, Harold tackled the electrical problem. Harold has a degree in electrical engineering and, with the use of my little ohmmeter, was able to solve the problem in a reasonably short time. He rewired the control panel and for the first time ever, I had both 110-volt and 220-volt circuits working throughout the entire boat.

We had planned to leave Bulgaria early Saturday morning and sail all the way to Igneada, Turkey, since Burgas is the only port in Bulgaria that we can check out of. The Turkish border was a long way away and we had to get an early start. When we attempted to leave Saturday morning, the Harbor Police told us that the Harbor Master had made a mistake and had not signed our final clearance. The Harbor Master's Office was closed for the weekend and we had to have his signature first. So we had to wait until

Figure 114
Dancers in Burgas, Bulgaria

Figure 115
Yacht Club in Burgas, Bulgaria

Figure 116
Stern view of Jon's boat

Figure 117
Street in Burgas

his office opened at 8:00 a.m. Monday. His office was two kilometers back at the tugboat quay. After that the Harbor Police had to come to the boat to inspect for stowaways and give us our final clearance after which we had to leave immediately! It was after 10:00 a.m. before we finally got clearance to leave.

When we were at sea, we kept noticing that the Black Sea actually looks black when seen out on the open water. We were not able to figure out why it looks black but that must be how it got its name. Later, entering the Marmara Sea, we noticed how blue the water was in contrast to the Black Sea.

Figure 118
Side street in Burgas

Burgas, Bulgaria to Istanbul, Turkey

Having cleared out of Bulgaria, we had to go all the way from Burgas, Bulgaria to Igneada, Turkey. Figure 119 shows "Idyllic" sailing off the coast of Bulgaria. Fortunately we had plenty of wind, but it was still after midnight when we entered the harbor and we were very tired. The small harbor was well protected and crowded with fishing boats. To avoid disturbing the other boats, we anchored out in the middle of the small bay and after a bowl of hot soup, crawled into our bunks for a good night's sleep in the calm harbor. We got up at daylight, made a large thermos of hot tea and left for another long day's sail to the Bosphorus Strait.

Two hours out on a 15-knot wind, an intense squall overtook us from the northwest with very heavy rain. Many hours later in the pitch black night we made landfall on a white light blinking 3 times instead of the 2 times that we anticipated. The GPS told us that this was not the mouth of the Bosphorus that we were aiming for. In close to shore, the wind died but the big waves continued. We rocked and rolled on down the shore with the engine. Finally we saw a line of freighters entering and leaving the strait. This was a relief after a hard day and most of the night on a stormy sea.

After entering the strait, we had to cross over to Poyaz Harbor on the other side. This was tricky as the large freighters and long tankers were lined up going at full speed into the strait on our side and going out at full speed on the other side. We had to time our crossing perfectly as we would be doing about 5 knots and they would be doing at least 15 knots and would be unable to stop or turn in less than a few miles. Just after one super tanker and just before the next, we gave "Idyllic" full throttle and turned to start across. Part way across, in front of a 1000-foot tanker coming at full speed, our engine quit!

Figure 119
Sailing off the Bulgarian coast

I dove below, assuming that the fuel filters were clogged again. Harold unfurled the genoa and desperately tried to catch enough wind to move the boat out of the path of the oncoming ship that would not even see us in the dark. There were high bluffs on either side of the strait blocking what little wind there was and Harold was just barely able to get us back out of the way in time, while I was upside down in the dark trying to get the gunk out of the filter.

We restarted the engine and this time we managed to get across between the ships to the harbor of Poyaz where we anchored about 1:30 a.m. for the night after 17 hours of sailing in stormy seas. Jon's boat that had passed us coming out of Burgas came in later that night and anchored behind us. They had trouble with their rigging and had been unable to use their foresail. The next morning we got up at daylight and left before they did.

Wednesday morning, September 1st, we had an exciting sail down the Bosphorus with lots of scenery on both sides; Europe on one side and Asia on the other. Figure 120 shows an old castle built to control commerce on the Bosphorus. There were two large bridges crossing the strait to connect Europe and Asia. At the south end of the strait, we passed by Istanbul, a city of 18 million. The strait at that point was very crowded with ships of all descriptions. There were many large freighters and tankers going up and down the strait. This traffic was overlaid with many crossing ferryboats and pleasure craft. I counted 17 ships in the strait with us at one point. Harold, at the helm fightingthe wind and the wake of the ships, wanted to know where the traffic cop was! Trying to keep a lookout and dodge the traffic was nerve wracking.

Figure 120
Castle on the Bosphorus

The other side of Istanbul, we went into the Atakoy Marina. This is a very large and modern marina with many pleasure boats of all sizes and descriptions. We radioed ahead and were met by a tender that led us to a slip near the marina office. The marina is very large and, because land is at a premium, had its headquarters building near the entrance out on the end of a long breakwater. Only the very large boats were tied up to this breakwater. The other boats were tied up at slips on the shore side. From the slips it was a walk of about two miles to the headquarters building all the way around the marina and out on the end of the breakwater. Unfortunately, that was where the showers and restroom facilities were located. Walking back in the midsummer heat after a cool shower left you requiring another shower. In addition, there was a fancy restaurant there and a large beautiful swimming pool with a bar on top of the building, overlooking the sea. These were all deserted due to the inconvenience. There was never anybody in the showers or the pool. The very large boats tied up near there had their own sumptuous facilities onboard. Figure 121 shows the slips and Figure 122 shows me in the swimming pool. This location seemed to be a poor choice by someone.

The small shore office had an Internet connection and there was a bus stop nearby. There was a pedestrian bridge near the bus stop to cross the busy highway going down the shore from the airport to the center of downtown. A large, enclosed, modern shopping center was just up the street; however, the prices were very upscale except for the large, grocery supermarket. There was also a large "Electronic Hypothermic Massage" facility near the marina with crowds of women in Muslim clothes waiting to get in. Throughout the day and night, we heard the "Call to Prayer" issued from the many minarets of the mosques.

Figure 121
Atakoy Marina slips

Figure 122
Atakoy Marina swimming pool

Jon arrived just after us and we joined forces to get our Turkish Travel Permits. This took the entire day, even though we used a young man from the marina office to do the legwork. The queue was long and the waiting taxi ran up a large bill that Jon and I split. I also had to visit the Customs Police to get a new visa stamp in our passports.

The next day Harold and I took a bus down to the Sultanahmet district to go sightseeing. We got off the bus at the plaza at the foot of the Galata Bridge that goes over the Golden Horn (an arm of the Bosphorus). The bridge has rail lines on top, an automobile highway on the middle deck, and a long row of restaurants on the bottom, pedestrian deck. Hundreds of fishermen lined the auto deck, hauling in fish just over the restaurants. Pedestrians were everywhere and autos horns were all blaring in the congestion.

On the European side, we visited the Egyptian Bazaar with its many thousands of small shops on a maze of little streets and alleys where we promptly got lost. We finally stumbled onto one of the many entrances to the Grand Bazaar. This is similar to the other bazaars except that it was roofed over in the 1450's when Melmit The Conqueror built it. There are 4000 shops under the roof on 65 covered streets. It is believed to be the largest roofed building in the world.

From there, we removed our shoes and put long pants on over our shorts to visit the Blue Mosque (Sultan Ahmet Cami) that is the largest in the world. Then we went to the Hagia Sophia (Mosque built in 532 AD converted to a church in about 1453 AD) that is almost as large as the Blue Mosque. After that we went by the Queen's Palace and later stopped at a tiny sidewalk restaurant to eat lunch on the way back to the bus stop. Figure 123 shows the Egyptian Bazaar and Figure 124 shows the Hagia Sophia. Figure 125 shows our route from Constanta, Romania to Istanbul, Turkey.

Figure 123
The Egyptian Bazaar

Figure 124
The Hagia Sophia

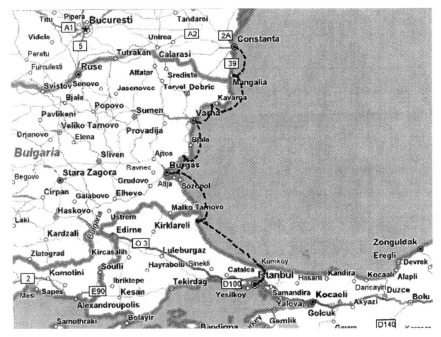

Figure 125
Route from Constanta to Istanbul

Istanbul, Turkey back to Yalikavak, Turkey

On Monday, September 6th, we sailed southwest on the Marmara Sea. Figure 126 shows Byler at the helm off the Turkish coast. Figure 127 shows some housing developments along the shore. Carrying strong winds and rough seas all the way, we went into the harbor at Marmara Ereglisi, Turkey, for the night. It was after midnight when we entered the harbor. It was very windy and a large swell was running. The small harbor was full of fishing boats and completely exposed to the high wind. We turned back up into the bay and went behind the point on the other side, which was somewhat out of the wind. We anchored there on a gently sloping sand beach in 15 feet of water. Since there isn't really any tide in the Marmara Sea, we felt secure there.

Unfortunately, we were broadside to the swell coming around the point. We rocked and rolled all night without getting much sleep, which we really needed having had a long day in rough seas. About 4:00 a.m., the rocking motion suddenly changed to solid thumps jarring the whole boat. We ran on deck in our underwear in the cold wind to discover that our position apparently had not moved but the fathometer showed only a little over 5 feet. The landmarks were still the same and we seemed to be the same distance offshore in the same place. We started the engine and I managed to haul the anchor up gradually while Harold backed us slowly back into the bay. During the night the current must have set us over a large boulder on the bottom.

I wanted to just go ahead and leave as we had another long sail the next day to Sarkoy. There really weren't any good ports in between. Harold was very tired and insisted on trying to sleep a little longer. We moved

Figure 126
Byler at the helm

Figure 127
Housing developments

over into a different part of the bay and anchored again in 18 feet of water on a sand bottom. The swell kept us from really getting much more sleep so we got up at daylight and left. We sailed all that day with a good north wind. It was a relief not to have to fight upwind. I always feel like we're in accord with nature when the wind is favorable. Figure 128 is a picture of me sailing the Marmara Sea.

Our next port was Sarkoy. Figure 129 shows the entrance to the small harbor where we backed up to the quay in front of the fish restaurant shown in Figure 130. Fishermen, and mainly the fish restaurant owner, operate the well-sheltered harbor. We had a good fish dinner there that we selected from an assortment in an ice-filled display case. The names of the fish are different in every country, so we just point at the ones that look good. I was out of Turkish lira but the restaurant owner exchanged a $100 USD bill for me. After the restaurant closed, we had a quiet, peaceful night and left early the next morning. Figure 131 shows us sailing the Marmara Sea.

As we left Sarkoy, we were starting to enter the Dardanelles Strait. There is a strong current flowing south through this strait. This current coupled with the strong northeast wind gave us 6 knots and better over the water; we were traveling at a high rate of speed. The wind kept increasing throughout the day and at one point, sailing with just the genoa, we got almost out of control. Harold called me on deck to help decrease the sail area. Even with only a small part of the sail out, we continued at hull speed. However, the wind kept increasing and we still had too much sail out.

The ship traffic was heavy and when we finally had to cross the strait, it became very tense. In accordance with the rules of navigation, we had been sailing on the north side of the strait close to shore to avoid the ships traveling at high speeds. Our next port was Canakkale, which is on the south side of the strait. Approaching Canakkale, the strait makes a sharp turn to the left, which put the 30-knot wind on our beam and heeled the boat down about 35 degrees with the amount of sail that we had up. Then to cross the strait, we had to turn even farther into the wind, which heeled the boat alarmingly. There wasn't any time to shorten sail as three freighters were going south with us and four were coming north to meet us. I waited for two of the southbound freighters to pass before making my cut. Unfortunately the 5-knot current together with our 6-knot boat speed almost kept us up with the 15-knot freighters. I pointed "Idyllic" broadside at the third freighter and we passed over her wake just under her stern. We could see the captain following our progress through his binoculars. I tried to cross in front of the bow of the oncoming freighter but had to give up and cross behind him. He was going too fast in spite of the current against him.

Figure 128
Knoll at the helm on the Marmara Sea

Figure 129
Entrance to harbor at Sarkoy, Turkey

Figure 130
Fish restaurant on quay

Figure 131
Sailing the Marmara Sea

We entered the harbor at Canakkale about 4:00 p.m. This harbor is adjacent to the downtown area and is very convenient to the city's facilities. We enjoyed the numerous restaurants and made use of an Internet café that we located. The weather was getting colder and the fall storms were starting. We got out of the Black Sea just in time. We had some bad, stormy weather with 45-knot winds right in the harbor after we arrived. The boat was bouncing so badly that we couldn't sleep. The harbormaster sat up all that night keeping an eye on the six boats tied up to his dock. He was a very conscientious person. One day when Harold was about to throw an old broken, worn-out pair of deck shoes in the trash, the harbormaster stopped him and asked him for the shoes for one of his workers. The next day Jon's boat came into the harbor. They had fought the stormy weather all the way in. Figure 132 is a picture of me on the "Idyllic" at Canakkale Harbor.

Figure 132
The "Idyllic" at Canakkle

The local fishermen came in to our dock every afternoon to sell their day's catch. They assembled along the dock in front of their boats and the townspeople came to buy the fish. We also bought fish and enjoyed some fresh fish meals that I cooked.

We were tied up next to a Belgium sailboat, shown to the left of "Idyllic" in Figure 132, with two couples and one other man on board. They were traveling the world also. The next day, they invited us for coffee and we talked to them for a couple of hours. One man had served in a Belgium unit in the Korean War. He had been in the Division next to Harold's during the same time period that Harold was there. Harold didn't know that the Belgiums had a unit in Korea.

The wife of the owner of the boat was very upset due to the actions of the Turkish Coast Guard. Their boat was yawl rigged. The mizzenmast on the stern precluded flying the Belgium Flag from the stern rail, so they had rigged it to the top of the mizzenmast. This turned out to be slightly higher than the Turkish courtesy flag at the top of the lower, starboard shroud on the mainmast. In addition, the Belgium flag that they had was quite large. The Turkish Coast Guard had stopped them at sea and made them take down their Belgium flag. She was still mad! When they left the next day, she raised the Belgium flag to the top of the mizzenmast on the way out of the harbor!

Thursday, September 9th, returning to the boat in the afternoon, I noticed a smell of smoke in the air and some clouds across the bay in the pine forest. I saw a small stream of smoke rising over the mountain but I couldn't see any flames. We went out to eat and when we came back, about 9:00 p.m., we saw a large area across the bay in flames. We saw red flashing lights there indicating that the Fire Department was on the job.

The next day, Harold and I traveled to the ancient city of Trova (Troy) that had been made famous by Homer's Iliad. We obtained directions to the Dolmus Gare (bus station) and purchased a ticket for 2,500,000 TL each. We found the dolmus with "Trova" on the front windshield and rode 35 kilometers through fields of hay, wheat, tomatoes, green peppers, and grapes spreading out in every direction. The admission price to the city was 10,000,000 TL. From the gate, we had to walk two kilometers to get to the excavations. Archeologists have excavated nine distinct civilizations there in different layers. Originally there was a port here at the mouth of the Dardanelles Strait; and in ancient times a lot of commercial shipping went through this strait. The prevailing wind is northeast straight down the strait. The ancient ships were square rigged and could not sail against the wind; so they were forced to anchor in this harbor to wait for a rare favorable wind that might not come for a week or two. Troy was founded in about 2000 BC to supply the ships anchored there. Then the harbor silted up about 500 AD and the city was abandoned. The original harbor in front of Troy now consists of a lot of cultivated fields. The excavations were very interesting. A lot of famous people visited Troy such as Aristotle, Penthesileis, St. Paul, and Alexander, in addition to the crew of the "Idyllic". Figure 133 shows some of the ruins at Troy.

Later, waiting for the dolmus to return, I noticed many wagons full of beautiful red ripe tomatoes going by. I asked for a price and a man offered to sell me a kilogram (2.2 lbs) for $1 USD. On the way back we visited a very large Gypsy market down on the riverbank at Canakkale. It covered almost a hundred acres. Figure 134 shows some of the local transportation. We had lunch at a hamburger place. A large hamburger with all of the trimmings and a Coke cost $.75 USD.

Figure 133
Ruins at Troy

Figure 134
Local transportation

The next day we explored Canakkale and found the Naval Museum in an old castle. Figure 135 shows me standing by a cannon at the Naval Museum. Figure 136 shows a large castle on the other side of the strait. We took a ferryboat across the strait to see this castle. These castles guarded the entrance to the strait, as this was a very strategic place. During WWI, the battle of Gallopi was fought in 1915 on the north side of this strait. Turkey had joined forces with Germany. Troops from France, Great Britain, Australia, and New Zealand tried and failed to conquer the Turkish army led by Admiral Kemal Attaturk. Five hundred thousand men lost their lives in the battle. Attaturk became famous as a result of his brilliant defense and was later President of Turkey. The inhabitants of the area still celebrate the anniversary of the battle every year. On the side of the mountain there is a large sign written in white stones saying "Mart 15 1915" that can be seen for many miles. Another sign on the side of the mountain titled "Dur Yuk" (In Remembrance) shows a picture of a WWI Turkish soldier. Figure 137 is a picture of the Lone Pine Battlefield and Graveyard monument. Harold left me here in Canakkale on September 10th and took a bus back to Istanbul to catch his flight back home to Texas.

Etienne du Bruyne arrived Saturday night, September 11th, after an 11-hour bus ride from Yalikavak. He gratefully came to help me sail the boat back to Yalikavak where I intended to haul it out and leave it for the winter. We went out for a burger before retiring for the night. On the way back we met some wonderful Swedish sailors on their boat "Barina" who have already circumnavigated the world and are on their second time around. The next day I took Etienne to Troy where he accidentally banged his head and skinned it on the Trojan Horse replica. The weather had turned colder and heavy clothes were needed.

Figure 135
Knoll at Naval Museum

Figure 136
Old Castle

Figure 137
Lone Pine Monument

We left Canakkale at 8:00 a.m. on Sunday, September 12th, and sailed briskly on a 20-knot north wind down the Dardanelles Strait to the Aegean Sea. From the mouth of the strait we sailed southwest to the island of Bozcaada. The harbormaster made us back up stern to the quay, which was difficult with the strong broadside wind. After a short exploratory walk around town we stopped for a cup of Turkish tea and returned to the boat. Etienne got into an argument with a local man who insisted on knowing what nationality we were. He yelled at us and told us that he was going to report us to the Coast Guard, which he promptly did. Nothing happened as a result and the Coast Guard didn't bother us. However, it made for a rather tense night.

I spent a relatively relaxed morning the next day. I went to town to cash a traveler's check. While waiting for the bank to open at 9:00 am,

I heard music that led me to the school. The children were all lined up singing the national anthem. The young boys and girls had light blue gowns over their clothes. The older children had dark blue tops over their black pants for the boys and Scotch plaid dresses for the girls. This was the first day of school for the Turkish children and their parents were all watching. After a few speeches, they all filed into the school.

The bank could not cash my traveler's check but did exchange a $100 USD bill for 150,000,000 TL. On the way back to the boat, I accidentally got bit by a large, playful, puppy. A policeman guarding the bank offered to help and wrapped my arm in a handkerchief. Sailing out that morning with a beautiful steady wind, we traveled fast and steady in crystal clear weather to Sevrice, a fishing village 48 miles down the coast. This wonderful sailing was quite a contrast to our trip up the coast.

While sailing on down the coast the next day, we were accompanied by about 50 dolphins. They jumped, rolled, and cavorted on the sunny side of "Idyllic". They apparently wanted to watch us without having to look into the sun. The next night we entered the beautiful harbor of Bademli Limani, which is entirely surrounded by mountains. It seemed to be a picture perfect, safe and quiet anchorage. We anchored behind a German boat in 5 meters of water over a sand bottom. I set the anchor well by backing on it.

The Cruising Guide warned of high land breezes at night so I let out more than usual chain just in case. Around 9:00 p.m. a strong katabatic breeze from the land started and intensified to Beaufort 6-7. Shortly we found ourselves heeling over on top of a sand bank with the wind broadside. The Cruising Guide said that the marine topography had been altered by the last earthquake in Istanbul, reducing the depth in places. We had evidently found one of those places. We remained stuck there.

Four fishermen came in from the sea for protection and I called them over. They said "yuck" (no) and "yarren" (tomorrow) and left for their seaside homes. There was nothing more to be done so Etienne went to sleep and I sat up worrying. I soon went to sleep and woke to a bright, warm sun and a very gentle wind. I could see that there was sand under us but there was deep water a few feet in front and behind us. There was a very small sand bar under the middle of the boat. Etienne started the engine and I tugged on the anchor chain and we came off the bar.

The next day we went into the small port of Siap. We had the place all to ourselves with a fish restaurant next to the boat. The owner let us hook up to his electricity. Etienne went to buy bread but couldn't find a store. We had an evening walk on shore, ate supper, and went to bed.

Next, we spent a very restful night at the Cesme Marina. We walked to town for supplies and visited an Internet café. However, all of the systems in town were down and they had not had any e-mail for several days. We left the next morning at 8:00 a.m. and ran into heavy seas right outside the harbor. We would have turned around and gone back in except that the nearby cape looked like it would offer some protection from the weather, which it did. Sailing along in relatively smooth seas with 30-knot winds was really nice until we came out into a large bay that was not protected. Etienne changed direction and ran downwind, which was tolerable. Unfortunately the only harbor in this direction was Pithagorio, Greece, that was 50 miles away in the open sea.

The farther we traveled, the higher the waves became. Finally we were beginning to surf down the waves. Changing our course at that point was not an option. We were committed and down the wild sea we went, up to 8 knots at times and averaging 7 knots skidding down the waves and hanging onto the helm. It was quite a sleigh ride! The gusts would heel us over with the bow digging in and taking a bit of green water with spray flying.

We arrived at the Samos Strait about sundown and rode the 5-knot current down the strait with the wind and waves diminishing. Soon we were going down the strait in pitch darkness. We were both familiar with the strait and with the help of the GPS, we found the harbor at Pithagorio without further problems. We anchored in the sheltered bay outside the inner harbor. After some hot soup and a hot shower, we went to bed around midnight. We had covered 78 miles in 12 hours for an average speed of 6.5 mph over the ground. That's not bad for a 32-foot sailboat.

Sunday we had a downwind sail all the way to Altinkum, Turkey, on the mainland. We anchored near a city beach in four meters of water over a sandy bottom. I swam a few laps around the boat in the crystal clear water for exercise. I noticed that the bottom of the boat was covered with green weeds and barnacles. The night before in the dark, I thought that I had

Figure 138
"Idyllic" at the mooring in Yalikavak

broken the shear pin on the dinghy outboard motor, but in daylight I couldn't find anything wrong with it.

We visited Didyma, which has massive pillars and is the largest temple in the ancient world. It is not recognized, as it was never finished despite centuries of construction work. A tour bus driver wanted to take me there but the dolmus only cost 2,000,000 TL right to the entrance gate. There were turtles, lizards, and rabbits scurrying about over the grass and marble blocks of the temple. There were very few tourists in evidence.

The anchorage there was poor as it's near several different discos with intolerably loud music all night. The south wind created a nasty chop in the bay. All of this made sleeping uncomfortable; but finally a transformer blew up and the electricity went off. Soon after losing their power, the restaurants started their own generators and the music returned louder than ever until the early morning. When we woke up it was quiet and the sea was calm.

On Tuesday, September 21st, we sailed to Yalikavak and moored to the large concrete block at the Tokar boatyard. Figure 138 shows "Idyllic" moored at Yalikavak. This completed my journey for the summer. Figure 139 shows a Mosque on top of the hill at Yalikavak. Figure 140 shows our route to Yalikavak from Istanbul. I sailed well over 1700 miles in three months of travel with half of it the wrong way against the prevailing northerly winds.

Figure 139
Mosque at Yalikavak

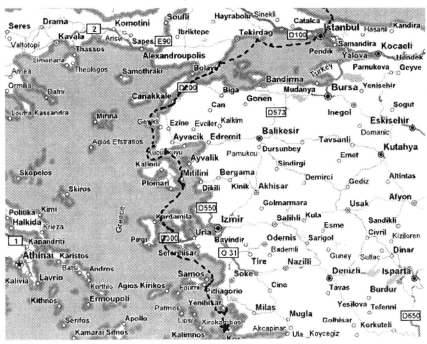

Figure 140
Route from Istanbul to Yalikavak

Yalikavak, Turkey to Michigan, USA

Wednesday, September 22nd, I went to Migros for groceries and stopped at the 3 Brother's Restaurant to visit Jemma and June. Later I walked to the Yalikavak Marina and bought 9.5 liters of gaz (butane) for 22,000,000 TL. It was very heavy and I had to carry it 2 kilometers back to the boat. Then I emptied and cleaned the clothes closet. I also took off some face panels to get to the bolts holding the shroud plates on and tightened these bolts. They seemed to already be tight but there was play in the plate. When sailing, I'd been hearing a clunking sound that had gotten louder and seemed to be somehow associated with the shrouds. This had been getting worse for five years and I wanted to fix it before something broke.

The next day I talked to Dan Smolen in Michigan who had been planning to come all summer. He has a pharmacy and had to find a licensed pharmacist to substitute for him before he could get away. Now, he says that he was having problems getting his passport but he planned to come on the 7th of October and leave on the 20th. I visited the bazaar while I was in town and bought some carrots, tomatoes, pickles, chicken livers, chicken breasts, olives, cheese, cabbage, radishes, and corn for 18,000,000 TL. I checked out the prices of tablecloths that were from 5 to 50,000,000 TL. Some were handmade but others were machine made.

Returning to the boat carrying all of the groceries, I was completely dry by the time I got to the 3 Brother's Restaurant, so I stopped for a big mug of Effes Bier on ice. Back at the boat I began the task of scrubbing the barnacles off the hull with the back of a wooden push broom. I looped the jib sheets over the side of the boat and secured them to the lifelines.

Then I donned my mask, snorkel, and flippers and went into the water with my broom. I could almost reach the bottom of the keel with the long handle of the broom when I put my head under the water. A large school of fish joined me to eat the remains as I scrubbed them off. After several dives, resting in between, I managed to get the hull fairly clean. I planned to give it a thorough cleaning later after I haul the boat out.

Friday night I met Clive Rogers and his wife, Collene, along with June Barnes and her daughter Jemma at the 3 Brother's Restaurant. We had Effes beer and lively conversation well into the late hours. Berk Ssker and his mother were there and asked to sail with me sometime. Clive is a bit of a comic and is teaching the Turks British colloquialisms such as "Bugger off". He is always playing jokes on people, so when I found out that he was planning a trip to the Temple of Apollo in Didyma, I asked him to pick up some of the little black Roman marbles lying around there. I asked him to bring me a bag of them. He said that he didn't want to get arrested for taking historic artifacts but I assured him that it would be all right if he asked the guards first. He took a bag with him for that purpose. He didn't realize that I was referring to the black rabbit pellets that were all over the place.

On Saturday I helped Etienne lower the mast on his boat. The varnish is peeling badly and he wants to spruce it up to sell it. His sailboat is small and the engine starts and runs very poorly.

The next Tuesday I walked to town and purchased three liters of diesel oil. My engine takes eight liters for a change. On my way back I saw some school children, shown in Figure 141, on the way to school. I stopped at the 3 Brother's restaurant for tea and they invited me for breakfast, which included tomatoes, cucumbers, olives, cheese, and bread with tea.

I ate out the next night at Mustaf's Restaurant where I had pork chops

Figure 141
School children going to school

that tasted a little off, but it may have just been the strange spices. After eating I had a nice chat with the owner, Brenda, an Irish girl now living in Turkey. From there I went by the Internet café and found that Dan was now planning to come on the 10th and leave on the 24th. This would rush my boat takeout as I planned to leave for home on the 27th. Some of the cleaning and bottom painting would have to wait until I return next year.

I saw June and her boyfriend, Tuna, who told me about their trip to Didyma with Clive. They said that he took the bag and went looking for little black Roman marbles before he realized what was there. Figure 142 is a picture of a typical Turkish toilet.

Figure 142
Typical Turkish toilet

Thursday, as payment to the boatyard workers who had hauled his fishing boat out, Mohamet donated a large bag of fresh fish for their lunch. One of the workers, Videt, made a soup with them containing onions, tomatoes, peppers, and pineapple in olive oil, which he served to all of the workers. There was also a large bowl of tomatoes mixed with green peppers, and onions and a bowl of yogurt. These two things were served in very large bowls. Each worker had a spoon and bread to dip in the soup. The 12 men, including myself, all gathered around the small table and empted these two bowls in short order without talking. We concentrated on the food instead of small talk.

I went to the market later and purchased five 5-by-8-foot hand-made tablecloths for 100,000,000 TL. I went spear fishing about dark to cool off from the intense heat. I shot a fish similar to a small shark that was with a school of fish in the shade under the boat. I cleaned and cooked it immediately. I tried a small piece then and since I didn't get sick, I finished the rest for dinner that night.

About 10:00 a.m. Friday while I was cleaning the inside of the boat, I heard my name called. I went topside and there was Jon whom I had left in Canakkale. I had suggested Tokar boatyard to him as a good place to haul out for the winter and there he was. I introduced him to Mohamet Tokar and we discussed hauling out his boat. Videt and I went out to measure his boat and found that it had too much draft for the boatyard sleds. They were unable to accommodate him so he sailed for Bodrum.

The next day a meltemi hit and lasted for several days. The "Idyllic" was in the best spot for protection from it but I still got short blasts of wind. I completed oiling all the teak wood inside of the boat and was getting very bored with the waiting.

It seems that no matter where you are in Turkey, there are many ancient artifacts. On the security fence I found a small amphora with the top and bottom missing. It had been found by a fisherman in his net and left on the fence as shown in Figure 143 for anyone who wanted it. I wanted to take it home but the penalty for exporting artifacts without permission is great. I talked to Dr. Ed Toksu, from the motorboat, "My Toy", about the amphora. He is interested in ancient Turkish history. He agreed that the amphora was very old and primitive pottery. The doctor was pleased with my loss of weight and said that he barely recognized me from last spring. We wandered over to the grave in the middle of the street and his mechanic was there praying over it. The mechanic said, "I don't care who lies here: Muslim, Christian, or Greek; but I still care and pray for him."

Figure 143
Ancient amphora on fence

Thursday, I went to the bazaars and stopped at the bank for 200,000,000 TL on the way. I bought the usual vegetables and several more hand-made tablecloths that I planned to give as Christmas presents. Figure 144 shows a farmer bringing produce to the market. I was overheated today and had to swim three times to keep cool

Both the old and the young Videts are working at the boatyard without pay. The old Videt receives an apartment to live in and food sometimes in addition to any work that the fishermen are willing to pay him for. The young Videt receives only tips and the money that he earns on the side. I haven't found an arrangement like that anywhere else.

Dan Smolen was supposed to show up on the 12th, so I waited all that day watching several taxis pass by without him. I finally went to the Internet café and found an e-mail there from him saying that he had landed on the island of Kos and planned to take the 4:00 p.m. ferry to Bodrum and then take the bus to Yalikavak. He had obtained a Turkish visa for $20 USD. Someone had tried to take advantage of him and asked for $100 USD. I calculated that, based on this information, he should be arriving in Yalikavak at that moment. I hurried back to "Idyllic" and he wasn't there.

I sat at the corner on a pile of eucalyptus logs, under a streetlight, so he would see me. After an hour a boy that I recognized from the Simge Yacht Co. showed up on his motor scooter and told me that an American was at the old harbor waiting for me. The boy called on his cell phone and handed it to me. Somebody named Carlos on the other end asked, "Where are you?" I told him Tokar Boatyard and he said that he would send a taxi with Dan.

Dan's dolmus had broken down on top of a mountain between Bodrum and Yalikavak. Passing Turks picked up the other passengers and left Dan sitting by the side of the road in the dark. Finally another Dolmus picked him up and brought him to the wrong Yalikavak Marina. Walking along the waterfront, he had met Mustafa Tokar, son of the boatyard owner. The owner of the Simge Yacht Co., who knew me well, had used sign language to describe me as an American with glasses and a big belly. Dan had said, "yes", and was sent straight to the boat.

Figure 144
Farmer bringing produce to market

The next day we sailed down to Bodrum where we took a tour to an old Turkish village 30 kilometers inland in the mountains. Sari Cigdem, the owner of Aegean Tour Travel, took us in her personal car to her home in the village of Comlekei, which has about 300 inhabitants. First we took off our shoes and entered the Mosque, built in 1401 AD. Our guide put a shawl over her head but wore jeans and a tank top. The walls were covered with Arabic writings. The Koran and the prayers were in Arabic with a Turkish translation. Figures 145 and 146 show pictures of the inside of the mosque. Figure 147 shows our guide and the ladies' section upstairs.

The people in the village are mostly untouched by modern civilization or foreigners. They work in the fields and tend animals much as they have done for centuries. They provide for almost all of their needs. They have electricity sometimes and a dolmus runs through town. Some houses

Figure 145
Ancient Mosque

Figure 146
Ancient Mosque

Ladies' section

Figure 147
Our guide

Grandfather

Figure 148
Woman boiling milk

have running water. The women cook over a wood fire, garden, and tend animals. Figure 148 shows a woman boiling milk. They raise cows, chickens, goats, and sheep but no pigs. The barn is attached to the house shown in Figure 149. From about the age of eight, the women weave rugs in their spare time to sell. Usually they make one rug per family each year. Modern steel looms are gradually replacing the old wooden looms that are then used for firewood. I asked the woman, shown in figure 150, if she enjoyed making the rugs and she said "yes" but her 14-year-old daughter, shown in figure 151, yelled from the other room, "I hate it!" This seems to be symptomatic of the younger generation all over the world. The profits from the rug go to the family treasury controlled by the male head of the house.

Most homes use about $10 worth of electricity per month but our guide's home, which has all of the modern conveniences such as air-conditioning, uses about $200 worth per month. With modern appliances such as a refrigerator and freezer, a back-up generator is imperative as the village system is very unreliable. Solar heated water tanks on the roofs, shown in Figure 149, provide hot water. This system works well since the sun shines there year around.

All members of a family sleep together on the floor in the same room. The 74 year-old grandfather, shown in Figure 148, had a bad back and slept on a bed. The 18-year-old son was in the army, which is compulsory. He was due to return in one month and his mother planned to find a wife for him at that time. Brides bring gold to the marriage and the groom must pay an equivalent amount of money to her family. The family buys gold with any extra money they have. They do not put money in a bank. The gold is handed down from generation to generation.

While we were in Bodrum, we visited the large castle there built to

Hot water heater

Figure 149
Cow next to house

Figure 150
Rug weaving

Filling jugs with water

Figure 151
14-year-old daughter

Figure 152
Bodrum Harbor

defend the harbor. Figure 152 shows the harbor and the harbor entrance. Figure 153 shows an Ottoman toilet in the castle.

On Friday, we motored back to Yalikavak in bright sunshine and practically no wind. Figure 154 shows Dan on the "Idyllic". We went first to the marina where I topped off the fuel tank for the winter. I purchased 92 liters for 160,000,000 TL. Then we went back to my mooring at the Tokar boatyard and made arrangements to meet customs officials the next day and haul the boat out on Monday.

Figure 153
Ottoman toilet in Castle

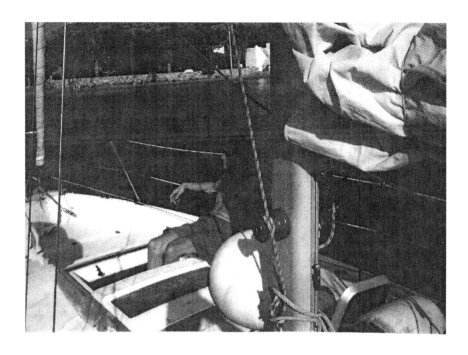

Figure 154
Dan on the "Idyllic"

That night we heard an explosion but nothing followed. The Muzzen then gave an extra long prayer over the loudspeakers on the minarets. We discovered that this was the beginning of Ramadan. This is a month long fasting observance with no food, no drink, and no sex between morning prayers and sunset indicated by the fireworks explosion. All three waiters at the 3 Brother's Restaurant participated, which was difficult for them, as they had to cook and serve food to customers.

On Saturday, I took Dan to Bodrum and over to Kos on the ferry, where I left him on the dock to continue his journey home while I returned to Turkey, where I had to buy another Turkish visa for $20 USD. Then I went to customs to turn in my Travel Permit and bond my boat to the boatyard for the winter.

Early the next morning, I prepared "Idyllic" for takeout but a large gullet beat me to the skids. I then had to wait the better part of the day for my turn. Everything went like clockwork when they hauled me out. The two Videts came at 8:30 and we removed the sled from under the boat using hydraulic jacks and propped the hull up with large tree trunks in seven places. Figures 155-160 show the steps involved in the primitive takeout process at Tokar Boatyard.

We stopped for old-fashioned tea made in a samovar. Immediately afterward I started to scrub the bottom, which turned into a hot job as the temperature was over 90 degrees and there was very little wind. I hunted up a ladder to put up to the deck and connected the water and electric. Then I took a cold shower to cool off. I pulled the dinghy from the water and washed the outboard motor inside and out with fresh water and then hid it in the boat.

Figure 155
"Idyllic" on the sled being pulled over the track

Figure 156
Greasing the track for the next boat

Figure 157
"Idyllic" on the sled

Figure 158
The sled to carry the boats

Figure 159
"Idyllic" on log supports

Figure 160
Knoll's home on land

The next day I had something stolen for the first time in Turkey. I had left my old worn-out sandals at the bottom of the ladder the previous night and when I came down the ladder they were gone! Videt recovered them for me from Effes, the guard dog. Later I cleaned out the chain locker. The bottom chain was a solid mass of rust that I had to break up with a hammer. I never use this much chain, but it is good to have as a backup if needed.

I had been invited to sail on "Funda", a Turkish gullet, in the Bodrum Wooden Boat Race on Wednesday but I couldn't find the boat amidst the marina full of race boats. That was a great disappointment for me. On Saturday, I unhooked the water hose and the electric line and stowed them away in preparation for leaving the next day. I gave young Videt 20,000,000 TL for helping me with the "Idyllic", as he is not paid by the boatyard.

On Sunday, I traveled for 12 hours across Turkey on a Metro bus to Istanbul. At the bus station, I took a taxi to the Sport Hotel in the Sultanamet District. I had stayed there previously and Harold Byler had stayed there on his trip home. This is a very economical businessman's hotel. The room costs $24 USD, which includes a large buffet breakfast on the rooftop with a beautiful view of the harbor. While standing in line there I met Omar, who is a Jordanian University Professor and he invited me to visit him in Jordan. I left for Montague, Michigan, on the 27th of October 2004.

Traveling is, to me, the unraveling of mysteries. Einstein once said that the most beautiful thing that we can experience is mystery. Mystery is the source of true art and science. My journey has been filled with the mysteries of the beauty of sea and sky, the wonderment of sunny days and starry nights, fog, wind, waves and storms of untold furry resulting in emotions of excitement, adversity, bravery, triumph, joy, and appreciation. I have experienced all of these things in my voyage around the world. When my "Idyllic" and I are in tune with the world's seas, then life is fulfilling and good.

I logged about 1750 miles on this leg in 2004 for a total of about 22,000 miles on my trip around the world the wrong way. The story of these travels will be continued in Volume VI of <u>Sailing Around the World the Wrong Way.</u>

About the Authors

Harold Knoll, Jr.

Captain Knoll was born and raised in Michigan, where his free days were spent fishing, hunting, and boating. His dream of sailing to foreign ports developed at an early age. He learned boating and sailing on Lake Macatawa and Lake Michigan. When he retired from teaching and farming, he began to live his dream of sailing around the world. Since then, he has sailed very extensively in foreign lands. He has sailed his 32 ft. sloop over 22,000 miles at the time of writing this volume. When he is temporarily home from his travels, he lives with his sailor wife in Montague, Michigan.

Harold C. Byler, Jr.

H. C. Byler learned to sail in the 1950's in a sailboat that he and a friend designed and built. He became interested in ocean cruising and recruited friends to rent boats and sail on the North Atlantic and Long Island Sound to Nantucket. He later sailed the Northeast Pacific, the Gulf coast of Florida, the Leeward and Windward Islands of the Caribbean, the North Sea, the Western Mediterranean, the Aegean Sea, and the Black Sea. He has authored several previous books and is applying this experience to assisting Captain Knoll with this book. He lives in a small town in dry West Texas with his sailor wife of 51 years.

Printed in the United States
113947LV00003B/178-183/A